Editorial Project Manager
Lorin Klistoff, M.A.

Editor in Chief
Karen J. Goldfluss, M.S. Ed.

Cover Artist
Tony Carrillo

Illustrator
Vanessa Countryman

Art Coordinator
Renée Christine Yates

Art Manager
Kevin Barnes

Imaging
Leonard P. Swierski

Publisher

Mary D. Smith, M.S. Ed.

Standards-Based · Grade 3

SCIENCE
Investigations

TCR 8963

D0557108

Includes
- Science Background
- Investigation Activities
- Inquiry Worksheets
- Standards Correlations
- Assessments

Author
Robert W. Smith

Teacher Created Resources, Inc.
12621 Western Avenue
Garden Grove, CA 92841
www.teachercreated.com
ISBN: 978-1-4206-8963-1

©2009 Teacher Created Resources, Inc.
Reprinted, 2019
Made in U.S.A.

Teacher Created Resources

Table of Contents

Table of Contents

Introduction

The *Standards-Based Science Investigations* series is designed to introduce the vital concepts of modern science to elementary school students in imaginative, effective, and easily understood terms. The series is carefully arranged to spiral essential science ideas through the grades, building upon the students' prior experiences in the classroom and in life. This constructivist approach allows students an opportunity to do carefully modeled experiments and then to extend these hands-on activities with investigations of their own.

Every investigation is introduced with at least two pages of instructional text, which expresses the essential science concepts of the unit in clear, simple, and correct scientific and age-appropriate language. The explanations are carefully geared to the students' grade level and the level of intellectual development usual for that age.

These introductions are expressly designed to enhance students' skills for reading in the content area. Reading comprehension of basic textual materials, content vocabulary development, and fluency are addressed in each of the chapters. The "Did You Know That . . . ?" statements previewing each unit are designed to attract and maintain the interest of the reader. Specific content vocabulary is highlighted in every unit and explained in accurate and easy-to-understand terms. Major facts within each text are highlighted and reviewed at the end of each unit in the "Facts to Remember" section.

After the instructional text, there are student activity pages. The activities and concepts chosen at each grade level are generally aligned with the framework and suggestions of the National Science Education Standards and match most state guidelines. Each grade level book has activities and concepts from the life sciences, physical science, and earth science. Many readings have important historical and biographical notes as well. The correct approach to scientific investigation is routinely used at every grade level with each increase in grade level supporting greater complexity and sophistication in science understanding and hands-on experimentation.

The Student Inquiry Activities at the end of most units are designed to provide several structured approaches to inquiry investigations by individuals or teams of students. They offer brainstorming suggestions and questions to investigate, which leads to the development of inquiry questions by the students followed by suggestions for getting started. Students will then pursue their individual inquiry investigations using the Student Inquiry Worksheets (located at the beginning of the book) to facilitate and focus their investigations.

In summary, the *Standards-Based Science Investigations* series is designed to make science literally come alive in your classroom and take root in the minds of your students. Enjoy using this book with your students and look for other books in this series.

Locating Simple Science Materials

Almost all of the materials used for investigations in this book are easily available at school, from local stores, or brought from home by students. A few science tools, such as magnifying glasses and eyedroppers, can be inexpensively obtained from science-supply stores. This page lists several of the materials used in the book and suggested sources. Supplies, such as scissors, paper, and rulers, usually available at schools are omitted from this list.

Materials	Suggested Sources
magnifying glasses	science supply
eyedroppers	science supply/drugstore
mirrors	home/science supply
insulated wire	craft store/hardware
bare copper wire	craft store/hardware
fishing line	general store/sports shop
flexible tubing	pet store/hardware
aquarium	pet store/home
flashlights	general store
potting soil	nursery/grocery
mealworm larvae	pet store
seashells	home/science supply
modeling clay	general store/craft store
balloons	general store
sandpaper	general store
measuring cups	science supply

Common materials available from home, grocery stores, and similar local stores

sunflower seeds	grocery/nursery
bean seeds	grocery—dry beans
wild bird seed	grocery
foam trays	home
wire hangers	home
blue plastic wrap	grocery
colored stars	general store
water bottles	home
clear packing tape	general store
food coloring	grocery
straws, stirrers	grocery
paper plates	grocery
salt	grocery
plastic zipper bags	grocery
paper cups	grocery
clear plastic cups	grocery
plastic silverware	grocery
pepper	grocery
aluminum foil	grocery
dish soap	grocery
rubbing alcohol	grocery

Standards Correlation

The K through 4th grade National Science Education Standards provide a powerful framework for employing the very best practices in science education. They provide broad and inclusive guidelines for the material to be taught in the physical sciences with special emphasis on properties of objects and materials, position and motion of objects, and light, heat, electricity, and magnetism. Education in the life sciences deals with the broad areas of the characteristics of organisms, life cycles of organisms, and organisms and environments. Earth science education focuses on the properties of earth materials, objects in the sky, and changes in the earth and sky.

The most fundamental aspect of the NSE standards, however, is its primary focus on the inquiry method of science instruction. Students use their skills in reading and in doing hands-on experiments to inquire deeply into chosen avenues of science exploration. They move beyond simple explanations and experiments with pre-determined outcomes. The inquiry approach is by definition open-ended and subject to unexpected results. It requires a good deal of rigor in applying scientific processes.

These inquiries have many facets. They help students identify appropriate questions for scientific investigations. They require students to design and conduct a scientific investigation that is rigorous, detailed, multi-faceted, and thorough. Inquiry activities develop the students' intellectual tools in gathering and analyzing data. They help students make predictions and draw appropriate conclusions. Critical thinking and logical sequencing are a part of the student's learning curve as are opportunities to cooperate with other students.

Students also learn to apply new technologies to their scientific learning both in the use of available computer applications and multiple sources of information. Students learn to internalize the essential contributions of modern science to the preservation of life and the protection of the environment. The broad range of modern science study is designed to make an impact on each student's life and his or her attitudes toward all forms of life. Students must perceive science as a human endeavor with a long history and great potential for making a positive impact on the future.

Instruction in this text matches all of these disparate strands of science education by providing important content knowledge, interesting hands-on projects, and challenging inquiry activities designed to help students internalize their learning.

Standards Correlation

Science as Inquiry (Content Standard A)
As a result of activities in grades K–4, all students should develop
- Abilities necessary to do scientific inquiry
- Understanding about scientific inquiry

(Units 1, 2, 3, 4, 7, 8, 9, 10, 11, 12, 13, 14, 15, 18, 19, 20, 21, 22, 23, 24, 25, 26)

Physical Science (Content Standard B)
As a result of the activities in grades K–4, all students should develop an understanding of
- Properties of objects and materials
- Position and motion of objects
- Light, heat, electricity, and magnetism

(Units 12, 13, 14, 15, 16, 17, 18, 19, 20, 21, 22, 23, 24, 25, 26)

Life Science (Content Standard C)
As a result of activities in grades K–4, all students should develop an understanding of
- The characteristics of organisms
- Life cycles of organisms
- Organisms and environments

(Units 1, 2, 3, 4, 5, 6, 26)

Earth and Space Science (Content Standard D)
As a result of activities in grades K–4, all students should develop an understanding of
- Properties of earth materials
- Objects in the sky
- Changes in earth and sky

(Units 5, 6, 7, 8, 9, 10, 11, 26)

Science and Technology (Content Standard E)
As a result of activities in grades K–4, all students should develop
- Abilities of technological design
- Understanding about science and technology
- Abilities to distinguish between natural objects and objects made by humans

(Units 1, 2, 3, 4, 5, 6, 10, 11, 13, 14, 15, 16, 17, 18, 19, 20, 21, 22, 23, 24, 25, 26)

Science in Personal and Social Perspectives (Content Standard F)
As a result of activities in grades K–4, all students should develop an understanding of
- Personal Health
- Characteristics and changes in population
- Types of resources
- Changes in environments
- Science and technology in local challenges

(Unit 2)

History and Nature of Science (Content Standard G)
As a result of activities in grades K–4, all students should develop an understanding of
- Science as a human endeavor

(Units 1, 2, 4, 6, 17, 26)

*All standards listed above are from *National Science Education Standards* (Copyright 2005 National Academy of Sciences, Content Standards: K–4)

Thinking About Inquiry Investigations

 IMPORTANCE OF INQUIRY SCIENCE

Reading about science is important because students should be well versed in the content and language of science. Replicating and performing science experiments designed to illustrate scientific phenomenon is vital to enabling students to understand scientific principles and properties. This hands-on science component creates an interest in and understanding of the physical world in all its varied manifestations.

The apex of scientific learning, however, is the inquiry process of scientific investigation. Scientists use this procedure to investigate the ideas, events, and phenomenas in science that they don't understand or haven't seen documented. In these investigations, scientists state the problem to be solved or the question to be answered. They design very specific investigations and experiments to test their own possible solutions to the problem or answers to the question.

 FAILURE ISN'T FAILURE

More often than not, scientists do not prove their stated hypothesis or even answer the question. However, most such investigations add to the information known about a subject in some way. It is important that students recognize that inquiry science and most original science experimentation fails. It takes many investigations to create a light bulb, to learn the living habits of an insect, to find a form of bacteria, or to map the migration range of a species of birds.

 SETTING THE PARAMETERS

Teachers need to set some limitations before introducing inquiry activities. These would involve sensible safety factors and limitations. Teachers should also set the specific expected behaviors required during an inquiry science period. These periods are often noisy and filled with conversation and discussion. Stress that discussions be pertinent to science and that all students must be involved and on task. Point out that investigations must involve reasonable topics and materials. Students will not have whales, elephants, electron microscopes, or jetliners in the classroom.

Thinking About Inquiry Investigations

 TIMING

Students need time to do inquiry investigations. Brainstorming, planning, and creative thinking are central to doing the investigations. In addition to building some of this focused thinking into the class schedule, expect some or much of the actual investigation to be done at home. Try to create a schedule specifying when each part of the investigation must be finished. You don't want it rushed at the end.

 GROUPING

This type of science investigation can often work most effectively with teams of two students working together on brainstorming and planning. Their exchange of ideas and suggestions often speeds up the early stages of an inquiry. They are often able to complement, motivate, and support each other. Groups of more than two students often have some students uninvolved or frustrated. Some individual students work really well on their own, and this is a good time to let a child work alone if he or she is so inclined. You may be better at choosing effective, successful teams than students will be.

 TEACHER INPUT

You need to be an advisor making suggestions, offering encouragement, and focusing attention on the project. You are a facilitator helping your students solve problems of logistics, available materials, and personality disputes. It takes a kind of light hand to keep kids focused on the task without telling them what will happen. Ask students pertinent questions rather than telling them what will happen or what can't be done.

MATERIALS

Children will have more trouble choosing materials and finding materials than any other part of the investigation. Help students choose reasonable and available materials. Give suggestions about possible substitute materials. You may need to help students realize they cannot do a specific project because there is simply no way to get certain materials or because safety is a concern. You will want to avoid dangerous chemicals, projects involving combustion, or dangerous tools.

Thinking About Inquiry Investigations

ACCEPT THE MESS

Inquiry science is often a messy experience with lots of materials and rather rickety constructions and models. If the investigations are done in the class, try to allow enough time each day so each unit's activities do not go on for more than a week. If all experiments come from home on the same day, devote most of a day or two to the investigations and presentations. Things are less likely to get broken or damaged if they aren't kept waiting too long.

ASSESSMENT

The rubric on the next page is a brief form with guidelines for the assessment of student work on inquiry investigations. It can be used as a checklist for judging the completeness of an investigation and the quality of the work. Students could also use it to evaluate their own work.

Be sure students know that they are not being scored on the success of the inquiry investigation but on the process. In these activities "Did it work?" is not the criteria. The adherence to scientific process, originality of thinking, data collection, and variety of approaches are the critical elements.
The final grade is based on the number that conforms to the general level of the investigation.

FINAL THOUGHTS

Enjoy the process. Encourage students to value their research and enjoy the inquiry experience. You and your students need to think of your inquiry investigations as an unknown path of adventure along the road to lifetime learning.

Inquiry Assessment Rubric

Final Grade: 4 3 2 1

Comments: _____

---

4 Points — Advanced/Above Grade Level Expectations

The inquiry choice and investigation demonstrates original and creative thinking.
The brainstorming for the inquiry topic indicates a diverse range of potential topics of varying value.
The investigation demonstrates detailed planning.
The inquiry investigation is rigorously and completely done.
Some kind of data from the investigation is carefully recorded.
Carefully reasoned conclusions are drawn.
The inquiry investigation worksheet is carefully completed.

3 Points — Proficient/At Grade Level Expectations

The inquiry choice and investigation demonstrates some original and creative thinking.
The brainstorming for the inquiry topic indicates several potential topics of varying value.
The investigation demonstrates fairly detailed planning.
The inquiry investigation is completed.
Some kind of data from the investigation is recorded.
Some conclusions are drawn.
The inquiry investigation worksheet is generally complete.

2 Points — Basic/Below Grade Level Expectations

The inquiry choice and investigation demonstrates some thought.
The brainstorming for the inquiry topic indicates only two or three potential topics of varying value.
The investigation demonstrates some planning.
The inquiry investigation is largely complete.
The data from the investigation is unclear or limited.
One conclusion is made or attempted.
The inquiry investigation worksheet is only partially complete.

1 Point — Below Basic/Far Below Grade Level Expectations

The inquiry choice and investigation demonstrates little thought.
The brainstorming for the inquiry topic indicates few potential topics.
The investigation demonstrates little or no planning.
The inquiry investigation is largely incomplete.
The data from the investigation is unclear and not useful.
No conclusion is made or attempted.
The inquiry investigation worksheet has little or no information.

Part A: Student Inquiry Worksheet

▷ **Note to the Student**

Inquiry activities are an advanced level of scientific investigation. In these activities, you design the problem to be solved or the question to be answered and the methods you will use. Some inquiry activities are to be done individually, and others by teams of two or more students.

▷ **General Topic (Examples: temperature, snails, soil, etc.)**

_____

▷ **Brainstorming, Ideas to Investigate, and Questions to Answer**

Write down your inquiry investigation ideas here.

1. _____
   _____

2. _____
   _____

3. _____
   _____

4. _____
   _____

5. _____
   _____

6. _____
   _____

▷ **Thinking with Pictures**

Make sketches, drawings, outlines, or designs to help you think of ideas to investigate or to go with the ideas listed above. Use the space below.

▷ **Assessing Your Ideas**

- Cross out any question or idea that is too vague or unclear to test.
- Cross out any question or idea that is too complicated to test.
- Prioritize your ideas or questions. Put them in order from best to worst.

Part B: Student Inquiry Worksheet

▷ **Choosing Your Inquiry Investigation**

Choose the question or idea you personally like best. Write it here.

_____

_____

▷ **Assessing the Investigation**

1. What materials do you need to do the investigation?

    _____

    _____

2. What help do you need to do the investigation?

    _____

    _____

3. Can you do the investigation on your own and answer the question?

    _____

    _____

▷ **Importance of the Investigation**

Why does this question or investigation matter? What will you learn from the investigation?

I will learn . . . _____

_____

_____

▷ **Stating the Problem to Be Solved**

State the problem to be solved in a question format.

Example: What materials will magnets attract?

_____

_____

▷ **Stating the Hypothesis**

State your hypothesis (scientific guess) while clearly indicating what you think will happen. Use a simple statement.

Example: I think that magnets can attract most materials.

_____

_____

Part C: Student Inquiry Worksheet

▷ **Planning the Investigation**

Planning is a very important part of your investigation. First, break your inquiry investigation down into steps or parts. Ask, "What gets done first? What part of the investigation comes next?" Then record the steps in your investigation below.

1. _____
   _____
2. _____
   _____
3. _____
   _____
4. _____
   _____
5. _____
   _____
6. _____
   _____

▷ **Making a Mind Map**

Scientists need to convert the pictures in their mind into a sketch, design, layout, or map of what they think an inquiry investigation is going to look like as it progresses from step to step. Make a mind map with sketches showing what you think will happen in each step of your inquiry investigation.

Step 1	Step 2	Step 3
Step 4	Step 5	Step 6

▷ **Anticipating Problems**

Scientists doing any investigation need to look ahead and anticipate problems they might encounter in doing the investigation.

Which step might be the most difficult to do? Why? _____

_____

What will you do to overcome the problem? _____

Part D: Student Inquiry Worksheet

▷ **Do the Inquiry Investigation**

This is the hands-on experimental part of the investigation. This part of the inquiry investigation involves using materials to make a model, gathering data to create a graph, or performing an experiment to prove a hypothesis.

▷ **What You Did**

1. State exactly what you did in each step of the investigation.
2. Draw sketches of the models and materials in the box below.
3. Record all data you collected in the "Data Record" section on the next page.

Step 1: _____

_____

_____

Step 2: _____

_____

_____

Step 3: _____

_____

_____

Step 4: _____

_____

_____

Step 5: _____

_____

_____

Step 6: _____

_____

_____

Part E: Student Inquiry Worksheet

▷ **Record Data**

Record numerical and statistical information in the "Data Record" section below. This data might be temperatures, lengths, weights, personal preferences, amounts, or anything that can be measured. Dates and times are also important.

▷ **Data Record**

Date/Time   **Data**

_____   _____

_____   _____

_____   _____

_____   _____

_____   _____

_____   _____

_____   _____

▷ **Graphing Results**

Some statistics are much more effectively presented on graph paper. Use graph paper to make a bar or line graph of the data you gathered.

▷ **Drawing Conclusions**

Did you prove your hypothesis? Explain.

_____

_____

What went wrong?

_____

_____

What would you do differently another time? Why?

_____

_____

What did you learn from this investigation?

_____

_____

Part F: Student Inquiry Worksheet

▷Science Journal

Scientists do written reports about their investigations so that other scientists and interested people can know what they did, how they did it, and what they learned. Write a complete report in the journal entry about your inquiry investigation for your fellow scientists (students and teacher). Be sure to stress what you learned and how the investigation was done.

▷Journal Entry

_____

_____

_____

_____

_____

_____

_____

_____

_____

_____

_____

_____

_____

_____

_____

_____

_____

_____

_____

_____

_____

▷Illustrations

Include any illustrations, pictures, or models that you wish.

Unit 1

Seeds and Plants

WHAT IS A SEED?

Seeds are packages of life. They are the structures used by most plants to reproduce. Inside each seed there is a young, living plant called an **embryo** and food for the embryo to grow into a plant when it germinates. The food is often packed around the embryo, but it can often be stored inside the embryo as it is with beans and peas. A tough shell surrounds the seed and protects the embryo.

STRUCTURE

The seeds of flowering plants can be divided into two groups by the structure inside the seed. A seed can have either one seed leaf, called a **cotyledon**, or two. Grasses, onions, lilies, palms, and many narrow-leafed plants have one cotyledon. In addition, cereals such as barley, wheat, oats, and rice have one cotyledon. All of these are called **monocots**. Corn is a kind of grass, and its seed has one cotyledon. It is a monocot.

Monocot Seed Structure

Many trees, herbs, shrubs, and beans have two cotyledons or seed leaves. They are called **dicots**. These cotyledons, or seed leaves, contain food for the plant to use until it is growing well in the soil and able to make its own food. Some pine trees and other conifers have many cotyledons.

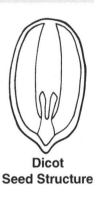

Dicot Seed Structure

GERMINATION

Seeds need moisture, warmth, and oxygen to grow. The process by which a seed sprouts is called **germination**. The first stage of germination is for the seed to absorb water. Temperature is important to the growth of seeds. They need either the warmth of the Sun's rays heating the soil or the warmth of a plant nursery, a house, or a classroom. Seeds of different plants need different temperatures to allow the seeds to grow. Oxygen is also important. One of the reasons planting soil needs to be loose and soft is so that the embryo can obtain oxygen.

Seeds and Plants

GROWTH

As a seed germinates, the cells divide and the embryo enlarges. The outer shell of the seed splits apart, and the new plant begins to develop. Once a seed has germinated, it starts to grow and many changes occur. The root swells up and breaks through the seed coat. The root pushes down into the soil where it starts absorbing water and minerals from the soil for the embryo. The stored food within the seed is used by the new plant. The shoot or stem grows upward. When this stem reaches the sunlight, it turns green and leaves start to form. The plant begins to make its own food. When the green plant makes food, we call this **photosynthesis**.

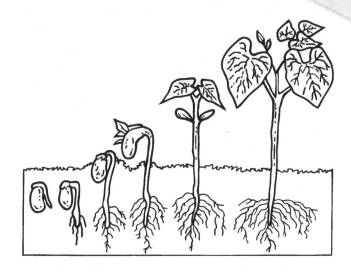

PHOTOSYNTHESIS

Chlorophyll is the green coloring material in plants. It absorbs sunlight and uses this energy to start the plant's food production. Plants combine water from the soil and carbon dioxide from the air to create a kind of sugar. The leaves give off oxygen during the process. The chlorophyll is unaffected and keeps absorbing sunlight to power the plant's "food-making factories."

Facts to Remember

- *There are two general types of seeds: monocots and dicots.*

- *The early stages of a seed's growth are called germination.*

- *All green plants make their own food through photosynthesis.*

- *Germination requires warmth, water, and oxygen.*

VOCABULARY

chlorophyll—*the green color in plants*

cotyledon—*a seed leaf*

dicot—*seed with two seed leaves*

embryo—*living plant within a seed*

germination—*process by which a seed starts to grow*

monocot—*seed with one seed leaf*

photosynthesis—*the process by which a green plant makes its own food*

Hydroponic Gardening

Growing seeds in water is called *hydroponic gardening*. You can grow seeds in water without dirt because a seed provides its own food during the process of germination.

Materials
- *bean seeds*
- *sunflower seeds*
- *clear cup*
- *white paper towels*
- *water*
- *measuring cup*

Directions

1. Examine one bean seed. Find the germ spot where the embryo will begin growing.
2. Examine one sunflower seed. Find the germ spot where the sunflower seed will begin to germinate.
3. Fill one clear cup with white paper towels.
4. Place three bean seeds along one side of the cup between the clear plastic and the paper towels. Keep the seeds halfway between the top and bottom of the cup.
5. Place three sunflower seeds along the other side of the cup between the clear plastic and the paper towels. Keep the seeds halfway between the top and bottom of the cup.
6. Slowly pour one ounce of water into the paper towels in the cup. Allow the water to seep into the paper towels gradually and soak it. Make sure the seeds are next to the wet towels. Add water as needed.

sunflower seed

bean seed

Watching Germination

Examine your cup of seeds every day. Observe and record the changes to the seeds. Illustrate one seed's growth each day.

Observations	Illustrations

Day 1: _____

_____

_____

Day 2: _____

_____

_____

Day 3: _____

_____

_____

Day 4: _____

_____

_____

Day 5: _____

_____

_____

More Hydroponic Gardening

Growing Seeds on a Brick

Materials
- *brick*   • *foam tray*   • *grass seeds*   • *measuring cup*   • *water*

Directions

1. Place a brick inside a foam tray. Pour 3 to 4 ounces of water into the tray until it is almost full.

2. Cover the dry top face of the brick with grass seeds.

3. Keep the tray filled with water for several days.

4. Examine the seeds on the brick every day.

5. Record the results here.

Date planted: _____

Date of germination for first seeds: _____

Number of seeds that germinated: _____

Number of days the seedlings lived: _____

Growing Seeds on a Tray

Materials
- *foam tray*   • *white paper towels*   • *measuring cup*   • *birdseed*   • *water*

Directions

1. Cover the bottom of a foam tray with two layers of white paper towels.

2. Spread birdseed over the paper towels.

3. Cover one half of the tray and seeds with a single layer of paper towel.

4. Carefully pour about 1 to 2 ounces of water over the seed-covered paper towel until it is soaked. Add water daily as needed to keep the paper towel damp.

5. Examine the seed tray daily. Record the results below.

Date planted: _____

Date of germination for first seeds: _____

Number of seeds that germinated: _____

Number of days the seedlings lived: _____

Did the seeds under the paper grow as well as those above? _____

How high did the tallest seeds grow? _____

Illustrate several seedlings on another piece of paper.

Measuring Using Inches

It is very important in science to record accurate measurements. One side of a ruler is marked in inches and fractions of an inch. Rulers usually are marked right from the edge of the wood but a few have an extra piece before the 0 mark. Be sure to place the end of the ruler or the line at 0 at one end of the object. Study the ruler pictured below. Notice where the half-inch marks are located. Notice where the quarter-inch marks are located.

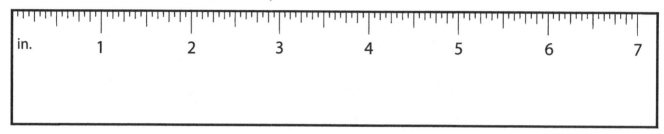

Directions: Use a classroom ruler or cut out the ruler pictured above to measure the length of these objects to the nearest inch. Record the measurement next to each item. Remember to place the end of the ruler or the line at 0 at one end of the object.

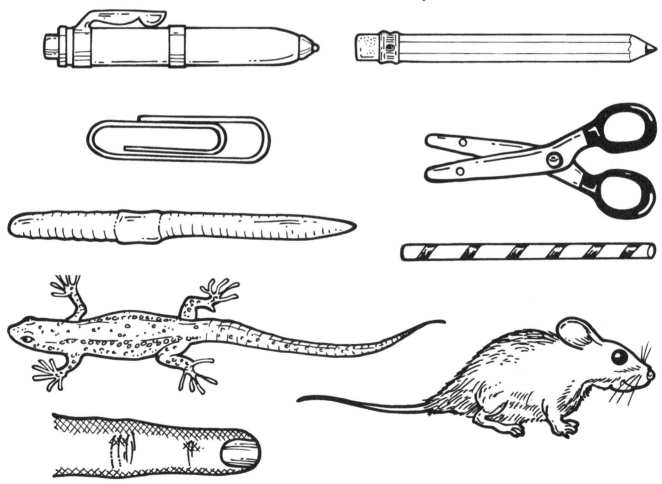

Directions: Now measure the same objects to the nearest half inch or quarter inch. Record the answers next to your first measurements.

Measuring Using Centimeters and Millimeters

You can make very exact measurements using centimeters and millimeters. One side of a ruler is marked in centimeters and millimeters. Rulers usually are marked right from the edge of the wood, but a few have an extra piece before the 0 mark. Be sure to place the end of the ruler or the line at 0 at one end of the object. Study the ruler pictured here. Notice where the centimeter marks are numbered. Remember that every tiny line between the numbers represents one millimeter.

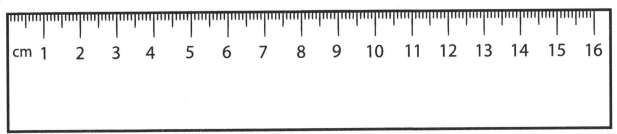

Directions: Use a classroom metric ruler or cut out the metric ruler pictured above to measure the length of these objects to the nearest centimeter. Record the measurement next to each item. Remember to place the end of the ruler or the line at 0 at one end of the object.

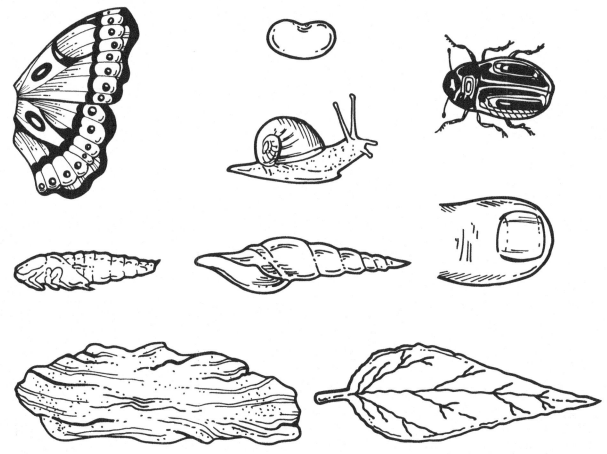

Directions: Now measure the same objects to the nearest millimeter. Record the answers next to your first measurements.

Student Inquiry Activity

Use this worksheet for a guideline as you complete this inquiry activity.

Questions to Think About

- How many different and unusual seeds can you find in your neighborhood?
- Do all plants in your neighborhood produce seeds you can find?
- Do all seeds need warmth to germinate?
- Do some seeds sprout faster in darkness than in light?
- How long will seeds live in water without soil?
- Will bean seeds grow faster indoors or outdoors?
- What happens to green plants without light?
- Which seeds grow best hydroponically?
- Which seeds grow longest hydroponically?
- Which seeds won't grow at all hydroponically?

Becoming Seed Scientists

Study the questions listed above. Think of other similar questions you could ask about seeds or plants. Write your questions here.

1. _____
2. _____
3. _____
4. _____

Discuss your questions with a classmate. Add interesting questions to your list suggested during your discussion.

1. _____
2. _____
3. _____
4. _____

Getting Started

1. Examine all of the ideas for inquiry investigation from your lists and the list at the top of the page.

2. Cross out the questions you can't do.

3. Cross out the questions that don't seem very interesting to you.

4. Circle the most interesting inquiry questions.

Do the Investigation

Use the Student Inquiry Worksheets to complete your inquiry investigation.

Ecosystems

DID YOU KNOW THAT . . . ?

- *An ecosystem can be as small as a rotting log or as large as the entire forest.*
- *Most plants and animals in an ecosystem, including humans, are composed of about 75 percent water.*
- *One small rainforest in Malaysia has about 750 species of trees. The entire continent of North America has only 700 species of trees.*
- *Parts of the Atacama Desert in Chile have not had rain in 400 years.*

THE BIOSPHERE

The entire living world on Earth is called the **biosphere**. This biosphere covers the whole surface of Earth and includes even the **atmosphere**. Every part of the biosphere interacts with or is affected, directly or indirectly, by actions in other parts of the biosphere.

The interconnectedness of life on Earth means that small changes in the temperature of one area of the Pacific Ocean may affect climate, plant growth, and animal life across large parts of Earth. A drought in Africa can change life half a world away. Minor changes in temperature can alter the growth of grasses, reduce the population of a species of mammal, and make an insect **extinct** in an area. Everything in the biosphere is affected by everything else. The study of the relationships between organisms and their environment is called **ecology**.

ECOSYSTEMS AND BIOMES

An **ecosystem** is a specific area of the biosphere that contains living things. It includes the soil, rocks, plants, animals, and the air in a given area. An ecosystem is a community of living and nonliving things. Ecosystems include forests, deserts, oceans, rivers, lakes, grasslands, seashores, tundra, towns, cities, farms, and mountains. They can cover vast areas or be as small as a drop of water, a child's **vivarium** (a place where living things are kept), a single human body, a tree, or a garden. They all contain living things that interact with each other and are different from their surroundings.

Very large ecosystems are called **biomes**. These include **tropical** rain forests, deserts, oceans, huge grasslands, huge hardwood forests, and similar areas. Biomes often have enormous influence over smaller ecosystems within or near them. They can affect the entire world. The destruction of tropical rain forests leads to the extinction of many species and different weather patterns at the equator and throughout the biosphere. Melting glaciers in the polar biomes will affect ocean levels and life throughout the planet.

Unit 2

Ecosystems

HABITATS AND NICHES

Ecosystems have many smaller **habitats** or communities of living things existing within them. A group of trees may form a habitat within an ecosystem. This habitat may include deer, rabbits, hawks, insects, and grasses. The habitat is the specific area where a plant or animal lives. The habitat is the address of a plant or animal within the larger ecosystem.

A **niche** is the role or job of a single living species of plants or animals within an ecosystem. The niche refers to the basic lifestyle of a plant or animal. The niche is where the plant or animal lives, what it eats, how it relates to other elements of the environment, when or if it reproduces, and even how it dies.

ECOSYSTEMS AROUND THE WORLD

The four major oceans of Earth are one giant interrelated ecosystem. Together they affect the climate and life of all other ecosystems. Each ocean supports many smaller ecosystems, habitats, and niches. Wetland ecosystems include lagoons, marshes, bogs, and inlets with either freshwater or saltwater. Tropical rain forests grow along the equator in Central and South America, Africa, and in parts of Asia. These hot, wet tropics are home to an enormous diversity of plant and animal life in many smaller ecosystems and habitats. Deserts are hot, dry ecosystems found on most continents. Mountains are ecosystems found on all continents. They feature a variety of habitats. Seashores are fragile ecosystems found along the edges of continents.

habitat

niche

Facts to Remember

- *The biosphere includes the entire Earth and its atmosphere.*
- *An ecosystem is a specific area in the biosphere.*

VOCABULARY

atmosphere—*the layer of gasses surrounding Earth*

biome—*very large ecosystem*

biosphere—*entire living world on Earth*

ecology—*the study of the environment and ecosystems*

ecosystem—*specific area of the biosphere*

extinct—*the death of a species of plant or animal*

habitat—*the home of a community of living things*

niche—*the role of a living thing within an ecosystem*

tropical—*hot and wet climate*

vivarium—*a place to keep a closed ecosystem for small plants and animals*

Creating a Mini Ecosystem (Vivarium)

Materials
- *aquarium*
- *grass seeds*
- *grass sod*
- *bugs (snails, spiders, worms)*
- *sticks*
- *bark*
- *jar lid*
- *water*
- *birdseed*
- *clear, plastic wrap or cloth*
- *small animals (toad, small lizard)*
- *garden soil*
- *leaves*
- *mealworms*

Directions

1. Use an old aquarium for this project. It does not have to be watertight.

2. Use a piece of screening, clear plastic wrap, or cloth to cover the top. Poke small air holes if needed.

3. Spread some garden soil or potting soil on the bottom of the aquarium about one to two inches deep.

4. Plant some grass seeds, spread some birdseed, and/ or place a clump of grass sod on the loose soil.

5. Add small sticks, pieces of bark, and several leaves to the ecosystem.

6. Place a flat jar lid upside down in the container and fill the lid with water. Keep it filled each day.

7. Add crickets, snails, worms, bugs, beetles, spiders, and other similar creatures to the ecosystem. You might try a small lizard or toad if there are enough insects, or you can add a few mealworms purchased from a pet store.

Ecosystem Observations

Draw a careful sketch of your classroom ecosystem. List, describe, and sketch each creature in the ecosystem.

Draw a second sketch of your classroom ecosystem a week or two after starting the ecosystem. Describe the changes that have occurred within the system.

Biomes Around the World

Directions: Write each plant or animal's name in the correct biome pictured below. Use the student reading page and other sources to help you.

polar bear	sea anemone	giant squid	dolphin
raccoon	fir tree	camel	jaguar
elephant	snowy owl	cactus	zebra
ostrich	orangutan	orchid	
Arctic fox	black bear	kangaroo rat	

Tropical Rain Forest

_____

_____

_____

Arctic Tundra

_____

_____

_____

Ocean

_____

_____

_____

Desert

_____

_____

_____

Temperate Forest

_____

_____

_____

Grassland

_____

_____

_____

Student Inquiry Activity

This page will help you get your inquiry activity started. This activity can be done alone or by a team of two students. Use the Student Inquiry Worksheets for a guideline as you complete this inquiry activity.

Thinking About Ecosystems and Habitats

What ecosystem, biome, or habitat could you study directly or by making a model?

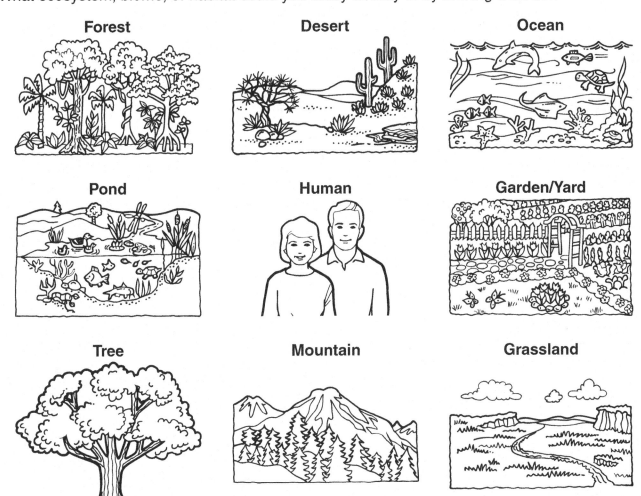

Forest   Desert   Ocean

Pond   Human   Garden/Yard

Tree   Mountain   Grassland

Getting Started

Choose one of the ecosystem or habitat suggestions. What question would you want to answer?

_____

What would you want to learn about that ecosystem or habitat?

_____

What materials would you need to study or make a model of that ecosystem or habitat?

_____

Doing the Inquiry Investigation

Use the Student Inquiry Worksheets to do your investigation.

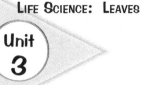

Unit 3

Leaves

FOOD FACTORIES

Leaves come in many shapes and sizes. They may be smaller than your fingernail or far larger than your hand. All leaves perform the same essential function for the trees and other plants on which they grow. They are the food producing factories for the plant. Without healthy leaves, trees and other green plants will not thrive, grow, or survive.

PHOTOSYNTHESIS

Photosynthesis is the scientific name for the process by which leaves produce food. These are the four ingredients of this chemical process:

> **chlorophyll**—a green pigment found in plants
> **sunlight**—the basic source of energy
> **carbon dioxide** (chemical name CO_2)—a compound of carbon and oxygen
> **water** (chemical name H_2O)—a compound of hydrogen and oxygen

Leaves need all of these ingredients to create the food that plants need to grow. Photosynthesis combines energy from sunlight with the green chlorophyll in the plant. This energy is used to make sugar for the plant using carbon dioxide from the air and water from the soil. The sugar becomes the lifeblood and food supply for the plant.

STOMATA

Photosynthesis occurs inside leaf cells that are packed with chlorophyll. Very tiny holes, called **stomata**, are located primarily on the underside of the leaf. These tiny breathing holes can open and close. They open during the day when the sun is shining brightly to allow oxygen and carbon dioxide to enter the leaf and water to evaporate. The stomata close at night or in very dry weather to protect the leaf. Plants living in dry places often have smaller leaves and fewer holes so that the leaves don't lose water or wilt in the heat. The surface of many leaves is covered with a waxy layer to prevent the leaf from losing too much water.

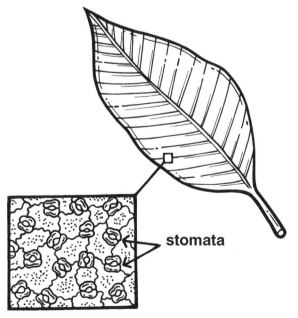

stomata

Leaves

LEAF STRUCTURE

Leaves are usually flat and thin so that they can absorb as much sunlight and carbon dioxide as possible. The leaf is attached to the plant by a slender stalk, which holds the flat blade of the leaf. The leaf is usually kept firm and flat by the midrib running down the spine of the leaf and the veins that branch out from the midrib. The veins and midrib carry water from the stem of the plant, and sugar made by the leaf is transported along the veins and midrib back to the plant.

LEAF SHAPES

Leaves may be divided into certain basic shapes. Leaves, which are shaped like the palm of a hand, are called **palmate** leaves. These leaves may have several fingers

palmate

pointing from a "palm" in the center of the leaf or several fingers branching directly from the stem. **Pinnate** leaves are shaped like a feather or a series of feathers branching off a long, central stem. **Needles** are the leaves that form on fir trees and other conifer trees. They may stay green all year.

pinnate

VEIN PATTERNS

Vein patterns in leaves can be arranged in several different forms. Many veins are arranged directly or almost directly opposite each other along the midrib. Other leaves

may have veins arranged alternately along the midrib. Some leaves may have a mixed pattern with some alternate and some opposite veins. Other leaves have arrangements that follow no set pattern.

Facts to Remember

- *Veins may be arranged in opposite, alternate, or mixed patterns.*

- *The shape of leaves may be palmate, pinnate, or needles.*

- *Leaves are the "food-producing factories" in plants.*

- *The process by which leaves create food is called photosynthesis.*

- *Photosynthesis uses energy from the sun, chlorophyll from the leaf, water, and carbon dioxide to make food.*

VOCABULARY

stomata—*tiny holes on the underside of leaves*

photosynthesis—*the process of making food in leaves*

chlorophyll—*a green pigment in plants*

sunlight—*the basic source of energy*

carbon dioxide (chemical name CO_2)—*a compound of carbon and oxygen*

water (chemical name H_2O)—*a compound of hydrogen and oxygen*

palmate—*shaped like a palm*

pinnate—*shaped like a feather*

needles—*multiple blades (needles) attached together in bunches*

Shape of a Leaf

Study the shapes of these leaves.

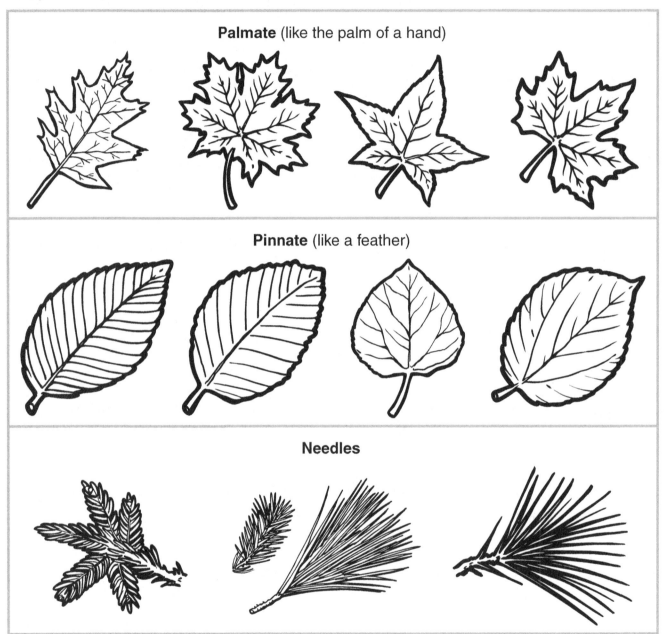

Palmate (like the palm of a hand)

Pinnate (like a feather)

Needles

Directions

1. Collect a variety of leaves from trees, shrubs, and bushes.

2. Compare each leaf to the illustrations on this page.

3. Make a pile for each type of leaf. Make one pile for leaves that don't appear to fit any label.

4. Use a separate sheet of paper to sketch and label each leaf you collected.

Parts of a Leaf

Study the leaf shown here.

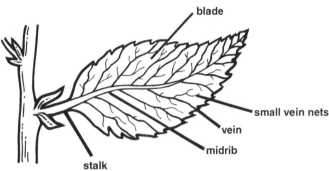

- The stalk holds the blade onto the tree.
- The midrib runs down the center of the leaf.
- Veins branch out from the midrib.
- Small vein nets often are seen at the edges of the blade.

Directions: Study two leaves from your collection. Then sketch each leaf in the space below. Label the parts of a leaf on each sketch.

First Leaf Sketch	Second Leaf Sketch

Vein Patterns

Compare these three vein patterns.

Opposite   **Alternate**   **Mixed**

Directions: Compare the leaves in your collection to the illustrations above. Place each leaf in a pile labeled "Opposite," "Alternate," or "Mixed." Choose the label that is closest to most of the veins in that leaf. (The veins in "Opposite" leaves will usually be almost but not exactly across from each other.) Make one pile for leaves that do not have one of the three patterns. Use the back of this page to sketch the vein patterns of your leaves.

Student Inquiry Activity

This page will help you get your inquiry activity started.

Getting a Feel for Leaves

Collect as many individual leaves as you can find. Then spread the leaves out on your desk. Look at them, study them, and feel them. Answer the questions below.

What would you like to know about leaves?

_____

What would you like to know about one kind of leaf?

_____

What was the most interesting or unusual leaf you studied?

_____

What would you like to know about the life of a leaf on the tree?

_____

Investigating Leaves: Inquiry Questions

- Are all leaves on one kind of tree the same shape?
- Are all leaves on one kind of tree the same size?
- Are all the leaves on a tree the same color?
- How long does a leaf on a tree last before it falls off?
- Do the leaves on some trees fall off easier than on others?
- Do insects eat many leaves on trees?
- Which trees have more leaves than others?
- How are leaves on flowers different than tree leaves?
- Do all leaves on one tree have the same vein patterns?

Write your own inquiry questions below. Then use the Student Inquiry Worksheets to help you choose your inquiry question and do the investigation.

1. _____

2. _____

3. _____

4. _____

5. _____

Mealworm Life Cycle

DID YOU KNOW THAT . . . ?

- *About one million **species** of insects are known.*

- *Three-fourths of all known animal species are insects.*

- *One-third of all known insect species are beetles.*

- *Insects have existed on Earth for about 400 million years.*

- *Cockroaches have remained almost completely unchanged for 300 million years.*

THE EGG

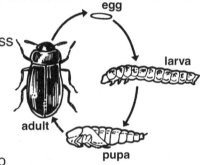

egg
larva
adult
pupa

Mealworms go through the process of complete **metamorphosis** in their life cycle. They grow and change from egg to **larva** to **pupa** to adult beetle. Mealworms begin life as a tiny bean-shaped egg about the size of a grain of dust and the color of white chalk. The eggs have a sticky substance on them and are laid individually or in small groups in grains and other foods that mealworms eat. They are very difficult to distinguish from the food and from the frass, which is the dry, white waste products they produce.

MEALWORM LARVAE

Mealworm larvae hatch from the eggs in warm and slightly damp conditions. They look like tiny moving fingernail clippings about one millimeter long when they first hatch. The larvae are tan, yellow, or light brown. They eat the grain or other food they were in when they hatched. The larvae grow particularly well in bran, oatmeal, and other cereal products. They do especially well in English muffins because they like to crawl into the many holes in this type of bread. Mealworm larvae need moisture but will drown in water, so they can be given raw vegetables, fruit rinds, sliced potatoes or apples, and similar materials, if you are raising them. They will eat damp cereal products but may actually die eating spoiled or rotten food.

The only way a mealworm larva can grow is to shed its skin, which is called an **exoskeleton**. As the larva grows, it swells inside its skin and eventually the skin splits away leaving a new, soft under skin that quickly hardens. Mealworm larvae go through between 9 and 20 of these larval molts before they pupate. Mealworms often grow faster in damp conditions with warm temperatures between the high 70s and 80°F. They do not do well in direct sunlight. Mealworms will remain in the larval stage between four to eight weeks until they pupate.

Unit 4

Mealworm Life Cycle

MEALWORM PUPA

When mealworm larvae have gone through several molts and reached a length of about three to four centimeters, they will go through the third stage of complete metamorphosis as a pupa. This is a resting stage, and the pupa moves very little. Mealworms do not spin a cocoon as some moths do. The pupa is a curled up, bow-shaped inactive insect. It does not eat. It turns from an off-white color when it first pupates to a tan, light yellow, or brown color like the mealworm. They may appear dead, but only dark brown or black pupas are dead. You can see that it is alive by holding the pointed tip of the pupa between your thumb and forefinger and gently squeezing the pupa. The pupa will wiggle and squirm. Mealworms remain in the pupa stage from about five to fifteen days. They progress through this resting stage faster in damp, warm, dark conditions.

MEALWORM BEETLE

The beetle will hatch out from the pupa quite rapidly once it begins to shed its pupal casing. The adult beetle is usually an off-white color at first but soon changes to a burnt red color and then darkens to a complete black in a day or two. The adult yellow mealworm beetle is a member of the family of beetles called *Darkling Beetles*. The adult beetle will eat but usually not as much as the larvae. The beetles live between two and four weeks. They mate and the female lays eggs, which eventually hatch out as larvae completing the life cycle.

The adult beetle has three body parts: head, thorax, and abdomen. The six legs are attached to the thorax as in all insects. There

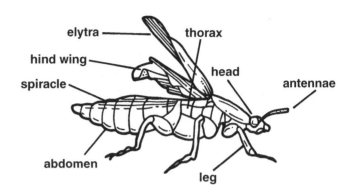

are four wings. Two wings are located under the hard outer wings called the *elytra*, which have many lines or grooves along the length of them. The beetles move slowly and don't fly. Beetles are more likely to walk on the surface of the food rather than burrow into it as the larvae do.

Facts to Remember

- *Mealworms go through four stages of complete metamorphosis: egg, larva, pupa, and adult beetle.*

- *Mealworms need raw vegetables for water.*

- *Mealworm larvae shed their exoskeletons several times.*

- *The pupa is a resting stage.*

VOCABULARY

exoskeleton—*an insect's outer skin*

larva—*the second stage in an insect's life cycle*

metamorphosis—*a process of change in some animals*

pupa—*the third stage in an insect's life cycle*

species—*one specific kind of plant or animal*

Mealworm Larva Observation

Materials
- *mealworm larva*　　　　　　• *magnifying glass*　　　　　　• *ruler*

Directions: Carefully examine your mealworm larva. Complete this observation page. Use a magnifying glass, if possible. Use centimeters or millimeters if you have a metric ruler available.

Description

1. Length of the larva: _____
2. Shape of the larva: _____
3. Number of segments (parts between the lines): _____
4. Colors (and shades of color): _____
5. Number of legs: _____
6. Where are the legs located? _____
7. Which segment is shaped like a triangle? _____
8. Length of one leg: _____
9. Length of one segment: _____
10. Number of brown or black dots or holes on each side of one segment: _____
11. Total number of dots or holes along each side of the larva: _____
12. Describe the feel and look of the skin. _____
13. Compare the underside to the upper side. _____

Sketch

Draw a carefully detailed sketch of your mealworm larva. Then label these features: legs, spiracles (breathing holes along the side), head, and segments.

Behavior

1. Cover your mealworm with your hand or a dark paper. Does the mealworm move away from the dark or away from the light? _____
2. What is the larva's reaction when you blow a light warm breath on it? _____
   _____
3. Have you observed your larva eating? What did it eat? _____

Mealworm Farm Observation

Materials
- *small, plastic container with lid*
- *bran, oatmeal, or other dry cereal*
- *pushpin or scissors*
- *raw vegetables*
- *mealworm larva*

Directions

1. Fill a plastic margarine container or small yogurt cup about half full of bran. You can use oatmeal or other dry cereal if bran is not available.

2. Place 2 to 5 mealworm larvae in the container.

3. Punch 10 small holes in the lid of the container with a pushpin or scissors.

4. Place a small piece of raw carrot, a piece of raw potato, lettuce, a partial lemon or orange rind, or other raw vegetable in the container for moisture. (Do not use water. They will drown.) Replace the raw vegetable when it starts to mold, rot, or is dried up.

5. Examine your mealworm farm at least once a week. Record your observations below.

First Observation

Number of larvae: _____

Can you find frass (small, dry whitish waste products) at the bottom of the cup? _____

Changes visible in size, color, or shape of larvae: _____

Number of shed skins visible: _____

Has any larva turned into a pupa? _____

Describe the pupa (if one is visible). _____

Has any pupa turned into a beetle? _____

Describe the beetle (if one is visible). _____

Second Observation

Number of larvae: _____

Can you find frass (small, dry whitish waste products) at the bottom of the cup? _____

Changes visible in size, color, or shape of larvae: _____

Number of shed skins visible: _____

Has any larva turned into a pupa? _____

Describe the pupa (if one is visible). _____

Has any pupa turned into a beetle? _____

Describe the beetle (if one is visible). _____

Continue further observations on the back of this page.

Mealworm Pupa and Beetle Observation

Materials
- *mealworm pupa*
- *mealworm beetle*
- *magnifying glass*
- *flashlight*
- *ruler*
- *pencil and paper*

Directions: Examine your mealworm pupa and beetle carefully. Use a magnifying glass and flashlight if available. Complete the descriptions below.

Pupa Observation

Length of the pupa: _____

Shape of the pupa: _____

Colors (and shades of color): _____

Describe the feel and look of the skin. _____

Compare the underside to the upper side. _____

Describe the pupa's reaction to light, touch, or warm breath. _____

Gently pinch the tip of the pupa between your thumb and forefinger.
Describe the pupa's reaction. _____

Sketch

Draw a carefully detailed sketch of your mealworm pupa on a separate sheet of paper.

Beetle Observation

Length of the beetle: _____

Describe the beetle's head. _____

Describe the thorax. _____

Describe the abdomen. _____

Colors (and shades of color): _____

Number of legs: _____

Where are the legs attached to the body? _____

Length of one leg: _____

Length of one antenna: _____

Number and shape of the wings: _____

Describe the feel and look of the skin. _____

Compare the underside to the upper side. _____

Describe the beetle's actions and behavior. _____

Describe the beetle's reactions to touch, hot breath, and light. _____

Sketch

Draw a carefully detailed sketch of your mealworm beetle on a separate sheet of paper. Label the head, thorax, abdomen, legs, wings, and antennas.

Student Inquiry Activity

This page will help you get your inquiry activity started. This activity can be done alone or by a team of two to four students.

Mealworm Inquiry Questions

- How are mealworms alike, and how are they different from another kind of insect?

- Do mealworms grow and change in cold environments like a refrigerator?

- Will mealworms grow faster at temperatures of 70° or 90°F?

- What cereals are the favorite foods of mealworm larvae?

- Which raw vegetables or fruit rinds are best for providing water for mealworms?

- How fast can you get mealworms to go through the four stages of insect development?

- Will mealworms live in soft soil with cereal foods?

- Will mealworms eat wet paper, tissue, paper towel, newsprint, or other paper?

Putting Your Heads Together

Read the inquiry questions listed above with a classmate or a group of students. Then discuss which of the questions you like. Discuss other questions that could be asked about mealworm growth and lifestyle. List three interesting questions below.

Inquiry Question #1: _____

Inquiry Question #2: _____

Inquiry Question #3: _____

Making Choices

Which question from either list most appeals to you? Tell what makes this question a good choice to investigate. Then use the Student Inquiry Worksheets as a guideline in doing the investigation.

First Choice: _____

_____

I like this idea because . . . _____

_____

Rachel Carson

Rachel Carson was a writer, a marine biologist, and the mother of the science of ecology. She was born in Springdale, Pennsylvania on May 27, 1907 and was brought up on a farm. She was encouraged by her mother to love and respect nature. Rachel loved to write poems and published her first story in a national magazine when she was 10 years old.

Rachel was an excellent student and decided to attend college, although very few young ladies in her time went to college. She was accepted at the Pennsylvania College for Women. Despite the fact that she received special scholarships, Rachel still had to struggle and work very hard to pay the tuition. She studied English and considered a career in writing. In her junior year, however, she took a biology course and was fascinated by the subject. Rachel went on to do graduate work in zoology at Johns Hopkins University in Maryland where she received her Masters Degree in 1932.

Later that year, Rachel got a job writing stories about the sea to be broadcast on the radio by the United States Fish and Wildlife Service. She took a civil service exam for a permanent position and was the first woman to pass the exam. Rachel worked for this government agency as a writer and a scientist for the next 15 years. She supplemented her government salary of $2,000 dollars a year by writing magazine articles about fishing and conservation. Rachel's father died in 1935, and she became the sole support of her family.

Rachel wrote her first book, a study of the ocean called *Under the Sea-Wind*, in 1941. It was not a best seller but was admired by marine scientists. In 1952, Rachel published *The Sea Around Us*, a prizewinning account of life in the sea. Rachel resigned from the Fish and Wildlife Service in 1952 in order to write full time. She published a second book called *The Edge of the Sea* in 1955. With the publication of these books, Rachel became famous as a naturalist, scientist, and author.

By the late 1950s, Rachel Carson was becoming deeply worried by the massive use of chemicals and pesticides on farm crops. In 1962, she published *Silent Spring*, a carefully detailed account of the dangers created by the overuse of these pesticides. She was attacked by powerful chemical companies, agricultural scientists, and some government agencies who thought she was scaring people unnecessarily. However, President Kennedy read the book and ordered a review of pesticide use. Gradually, it became clear that her scientific observations and information were accurate. Over the course of the next 10 years, private businesses and government agencies curtailed the use of some of these pesticides, especially the dangerous chemical, DDT. Unfortunately, Rachel Carson did not live to see the acceptance of her ideas. She died of breast cancer at the age of 56 in 1964.

Shells

DID YOU KNOW THAT . . . ?

- *Chalk is made from the shells of long dead mollusks.*

- *Most shells coil in a clockwise direction.*

- *Many snails and slugs are both male and female. Any two snails of this type can mate.*

- *Cone shells are gastropods that use poison to kill their prey. The poison in some of these living cone snails is powerful enough to kill humans.*

ANIMALS IN ARMOR

Seashells are the armor that protect a large group of animals known as **mollusks**. The shell serves as a skeleton to support the mollusk's body and as a shelter against weather and temperature. Some 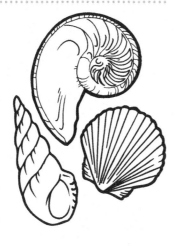 mollusks survive in desert temperatures over 100°F. Others endure freezing arctic temperatures. The shell is a mobile "home" providing strong protection against predators.

A mollusk produces its shell by secreting a chemical in the mantle, a layer of living tissue covering its body and the shell. This chemical is called *calcium carbonate*, which is the same material as chalk. As the body of the mollusk grows, the edges of the shell grow. A shell usually has three layers: a thin outer layer, a thick middle layer, and a thin, often shiny, inner layer.

There are more than 90,000 species of living mollusks and tens of thousands more that lived millions of years ago but are now extinct. Many mollusks live in water, but others, such as garden snails and slugs, live on land and breathe air. There are two main groups of mollusks: **gastropods** and **bivalves**.

GASTROPODS

Gastropod means "stomach-footed." More than half of all gastropods live in the ocean. These sea snails usually have a large, muscled foot, which they use for movement. They have a coiled or pyramid-like shell. Most gastropod shells coil in a clockwise direction. Gastropods in the ocean live in the water and breathe through gills. The **siphon** on the head of a gastropod pulls water past the gills.

Shells

UNIVALVES

Gastropods are **univalves**. A univalve has only one shell and stays in the same shell its entire life. Each shell has a hidden opening that can be closed off. The edges of the opening are called the *lips*. During times of danger, these snails can usually pull themselves into their shells. Gastropods include conches, whelks, abalones, murex, augurs, and limpets.

BIVALVES

There are more than 20,000 living species of bivalves and thousands more that lived millions of years

ago. Bivalves have two shells, which are connected by a tough muscular piece of tissue acting like a hinge. Some have valves or shells that look the same. Others may have different shapes. Muscles inside the shell and the hinge allow the animal to open and close its shell. Some bivalves, like mussels, rarely or never move. They glue themselves to a rock with a tough, silky material. Other bivalves push themselves along or bury themselves in sand using a hatchet-shaped foot. Bivalves have no head. They filter food out of the water with their gills. Bivalves include oysters, clams, cockleshells, scallops, and mussels.

CHITONS AND TUSK SHELLS

Chitons have existed for more than 500 million years. The shell of a chiton has eight hard, overlapping plates that are held

together by a tough girdle of tissue. Chitons live on rocks, in cracks, and in places where they can attach themselves tightly. They can curl up

like a ball if pried loose. Chitons feed at night on algae. *Tusk shells* are shaped like long teeth, and were once highly valued by Native Americans and used as a form of money. The living creatures have no head, eyes, or gills. They can be found buried in sand. They are usually whitish and smooth.

Facts to Remember

● *Shells are produced by a class of animals called mollusks.*

● *There are two main classes of mollusks. Gastropods have one shell. Bivalves have two shells.*

VOCABULARY

bivalve—*a mollusk with two shells*

gastropod—*a snail which moves on one foot*

mollusk—*soft-bodied animal usually covered by a shell*

siphon—*a tube used to bring water into a mollusk's body*

univalve—*a mollusk with one shell*

Examining Shells

Directions

1. Carefully examine two shells from your class collection.
2. Record the information below about each shell.
3. Use the Shell Identification Guide on page 45 to make a reasonable guess about the name of each shell. Use other sources in books or the Internet to confirm your identification.

First Shell

Length: _____

Width (at the widest part): _____

Outside Colors (and shades of color): _____

Inside Colors: _____

Texture (feel) of the inside: _____

Shape of the shell: _____

Gastropod or bivalve: _____

Name of shell: _____

| Front or Top View | Back or Bottom View |

Second Shell

Length: _____

Width (at the widest part): _____

Outside Colors (and shades of color): _____

Inside Colors: _____

Texture (feel) of the outside: _____

Texture (feel) of the inside: _____

Shape of the shell: _____

Gastropod or Bivalve: _____

Name of Shell: _____

| Front or Top View | Back or Bottom View |

Shell Identification Guide

Directions: Use the illustrations on this page to help you identify the basic type of seashell you are examining.

Bivalves

Clams	Scallops	Cockle Shells
Mussels	**Pen Shells**	**Oysters**

Gastropods

Conchs	Helmet Shells	Whelks
Murex Shells	**Tritons**	**Volute Shells**
Cone Shells	**Tulip Shells**	**Cowries**
Augurs	**Tegula Shells**	**Olive Shells**

True Limpets	**Abalone**	**Keyhole Limpets**
		—

Other Shells

Chitons	Tusk Shells

Fossils

DID YOU KNOW THAT . . . ?

- *Ninety-nine percent of all the species of living things that ever existed are now extinct.*

- *Dinosaurs, such as Brachiosaurus, could have weighed as much as 50 tons—the weight of 50 cars. Other dinosaurs, such as the Compsognathus, weighed about as much as a six-pound house cat.*

- *The coelacanth was considered an extinct fossil fish, which died out 60 million years ago until a fisherman caught one in 1938 off the coast of Madagascar.*

WHAT ARE FOSSILS?

Fossils are the remains of any living creature, from the smallest bacteria to the largest dinosaur. They may have lived a few  thousand years ago or many millions of years ago. Fossils may include bones, skin, shells, plant fibers, insects, or any physical fragment of a once-living organism. Compared to the number of organisms that have been alive, fossils are quite rare. Fossil traces, such as footprints, are also important evidence to the study of paleontology. A **paleontologist** is a scientist who studies fossils.

FOSSIL FORMATION UNDER WATER

Fossils are more likely to be created and preserved under water. A sea creature, such as a clam, mussel, or shrimp, will sink to the sea floor when it dies. Any remaining soft parts usually decay. The shell is hard and is gradually buried under sediment and pressed down by the weight of the water and the layers of sediment that form on top of the shell. The mud and sediment eventually harden into rock themselves. The shell itself is preserved or the impression of the shell remains in the rock. Leaf impressions and footprints are also sometimes preserved in shallow seas and shorelines.

FOSSIL PRESERVATION ON LAND

Animals that die on land are less likely to be preserved in the fossil record. Carnivores and scavengers that eat the rotting remains of dead bodies will eat their flesh. The bones may be scattered and broken by the strong teeth of other scavenging animals. The bones may be carried away by water, worn away by erosion, heat, cold, and blowing sand, or buried.

Fossils

FREEZING

Freezing may preserve some fossils. Animals who died in the last ice age may be preserved in glaciers. The cold may have been uninterrupted for 10,000 years. Some woolly mammoths have been so well preserved in Siberian and Alaskan regions that the hair, skin, and flesh have not decayed. The undigested contents of these animals' stomachs have been examined to determine exactly what plant life they ate.

SKULLS AND BONES

Occasionally, scientists and amateur paleontologists discover the bones or skull of a long extinct animal. Many dinosaur discoveries do not include a complete skeleton. Sometimes only a few bones and a skull are found. Scientists try to assemble what they have and guess at what's missing as if they were working on a gigantic and incomplete jigsaw puzzle. Smaller creatures are even more unlikely to be found entirely intact.

PETRIFIED FOSSILS

Petrified fossils are one of the most fascinating types of fossils. The living parts of an extinct organism may be buried in water with a heavy concentration of mineral salts. As the soft parts of the plant or animal decay, minerals in the water replace them. Petrified wood from forests that were suddenly buried in sea water provide scientists with an exact image of what the tree looked like when it was alive.

PEAT BOGS, TAR PITS, AND AMBER

Some of the best fossils of more recent organisms are found in **peat** bogs where they could not decay or in **tar pits** where the creatures are perfectly preserved by the tar. Dire wolves, giant sloths, and saber-toothed cats have been found in tar pits. The tar pits in Los Angeles have been the source of thousands of specimens that are on display in a museum next door. **Amber** is a sticky liquid sap that leaks out of trees. Spiders and insects are sometimes trapped and covered in this sap, which hardens over time. Scientists can then examine the perfectly preserved insects and other small creatures.

Facts to Remember

- *Fossils are the remains of once living plants and animals.*

- *Fossils can be preserved in tar pits, amber, and peat bogs.*

- *Fossils can be preserved under sea and by becoming rock.*

- *Some fossil tracks and bones are found.*

VOCABULARY

amber—*hardened tree sap*

fossil—*the remains of a once living organism*

paleontologist—*a scientist who studies fossils*

peat—*partly decayed plants from ancient swamps*

petrified—*to turn into stone*

tar pit—*a pool of tar*

Fossil Prints

Finding true fossils is often difficult to do. Use this page to make and collect fossil prints of objects that could become fossils.

Materials
- *nature objects, such as shells, leaves, bark, flowers, and bones*
- *small box, foam tray, clean milk carton, or plastic bowl*
- *modeling clay*
- *plastic resealable bags*

Directions

1. Collect as many objects from nature as you can. Use the following guidelines to help you:

   - Look for leaves with a large midrib and veins.

   - Look for rigid tree bark.

   - Search for flowers that have hard petals or seed cases.

   - Look for bones or parts of bones and shells from garden snails or seashells.

   - Look for feathers or the hard outer coverings of beetles or other dead insects.

2. Use one ounce of modeling clay. Mold it until it is very soft.

3. Smooth the clay into the bottom of a small cardboard box, foam tray, clean milk carton, plastic bowl, or any similar item.

4. Gently but firmly press part or all of one nature object into the clay. Remove the object. Press a second or third object into the clay. Overlap some on the first object. Complete the fossil print as you wish.

5. Put the fossil prints on display in the classroom. Put the specimens in a bag.

Recognizing Fossils

Exchange prints with one other student. Try to guess which natural objects were used in his or her print. Make a list and compare your guess with the exact specimens in the bag. Find another classmate and switch again. Try to examine everyone's prints.

Field Fossil Find

Go on a field fossil find through the playground, along the fences, or in gardens and fields. Take an ounce of modeling clay. Try to collect some field prints from tracks or objects that cannot be moved.

Galileo Galilei

Galileo Galilei was born on February 15, 1564, in Pisa, Italy. The family moved to Florence in the 1570s and Galileo's father arranged for him to be educated at a local monastery and then sent him to the University of Pisa in 1581, where he expected his son to study medicine and become a doctor. Education was a rare opportunity open to only a few fortunate young men.

Galileo spent four years studying medicine and the natural philosophy of the ancient Greek scientists. He was especially fascinated by mathematics. He left the university and tutored students in mathematics for about four years. He continued his studies on his own and even invented an instrument for finding the specific gravity of different materials by weighing them in water. It was his first scientific invention.

In 1589, Galileo was appointed professor of mathematics at the University of Pisa where he also taught courses in astronomy. In those days, astronomy was based on the ancient Greek concepts suggested by Ptolemy. This ancient Greek philosopher had believed that Earth was the center of the solar system and that all planets revolved around Earth.

In 1609, Galileo built his first telescope, an instrument capable of magnifying objects up to 30 times. He discovered that the moon's surface was pitted and mountainous, and he thought he saw seas. Galileo discovered four of Jupiter's moons, which are now called the Galilean moons. He studied sunspots and the phases of Venus. Galileo became quite famous when he published his discoveries. He would eventually be blinded by studying the sun with the telescope, which destroyed sensitive areas of his eyes by magnifying the bright light of the sun. Today, every student knows that you never look through a telescope directly at the sun.

Galileo also studied the laws of motion, especially those concerned with the movements of a pendulum and the falling rate of objects. He became interested in pendulums while watching a large candleholder in church swing at regular intervals. He did experiments to prove that the falling rate of objects was not affected by weight alone. He dropped objects of the same size but different weights and found that they fell at the same speed. Galileo was one of the first scientists to be concerned with proof based on the results of experimentation. He did not believe what earlier scientists claimed unless it could be proved.

In the course of his studies, Galileo came to believe that the new ideas of Nicolaus Copernicus were correct. Copernicus had written that all the planets revolved around the sun. This idea was completely opposed by the influential Catholic Church, which eventually tried Galileo for false teachings, and he was held under house arrest for the last years of his life.

Constellations

DID YOU KNOW THAT . . . ?

- *Many of the constellations were named more than 4,000 years ago by Babylonian astronomers.*

- *Light travels about 186,000 miles per second.*

- *A light year is the distance light can travel in one year—about 6 trillion miles.*

- *Nothing travels faster than the speed of light.*

Many ancient peoples invented names for the star patterns they observed in the night sky. The Babylonians, Egyptians, Chinese, Greeks, and many others recognized these patterns and created names from their cultures, including animals and people, for these patterns. The Greeks and Romans recognized about 48 of these **constellations**. The age of exploration led to the discovery of many more patterns in the Southern Hemisphere, in the newly explored areas below the equator. There are now 88 recognized constellations.

Stars in a constellation lie in the same area of the sky from an observer's point of view, but they are not close to each other in space. The stars in the constellation Orion appear close to each other, but they may be 500 to 2,000 **light years** away from Earth. This is a huge distance. A light year is a method of measuring huge distances in space. One light year represents a distance of about 6 trillion miles, so these stars may be 3,000 trillion to 12,000 trillion miles from Earth.

ORION (THE HUNTER)

In one version of a Greek myth, Artemis, the goddess of the moon and of hunting, fell in love with Orion, but she accidentally killed him. She placed him in the sky marked with bright stars. Look for the three bright stars which make up the belt of Orion. Orion is easy to find in fall and winter.

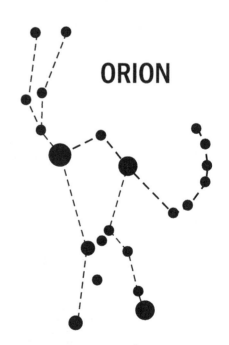

ORION

Constellations

CASSIOPEIA

In one version of a Greek myth, Cassiopeia and her husband, Cepheus, were rulers of an ancient kingdom. Their daughter's name was Andromeda. Cassiopeia boasted that she was more beautiful than the Nereids, the sea nymphs. They complained to Poseidon, their father and the god of the sea. Poseidon sent a sea monster, Cetus, to destroy the kingdom ruled by Cassiopeia. To save his kingdom, Cepheus was ordered to sacrifice his daughter Andromeda to Cetus, the sea monster. Andromeda was saved by Perseus. All of these characters are featured in other constellations. Cassiopeia is easy to see in the northern sky. It can look like the letters W, M, or E depending on the time of year.

URSA MAJOR AND URSA MINOR

To the ancient Greeks, Ursa Major (The Great Bear) was a young girl turned into a bear by Hera, the jealous wife of Zeus, the king of the gods. Zeus placed her in the sky with his son Arcas, who became Ursa Minor, the Little Bear. Both of these constellations are visible throughout the year. The seven brightest stars of Ursa Major represent an asterism called the *Big Dipper* or the *Plough*. An **asterism** is a distinct, easy-to-see group of stars within a constellation. Polaris, the North Star, is located at the handle of Ursa Minor, which is also known as the *Little Dipper*.

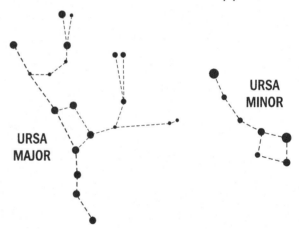

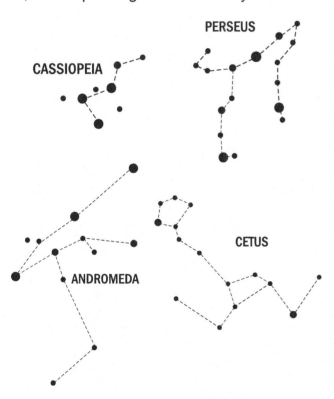

Facts to Remember

- *There are 88 recognized constellations.*
- *Distance is measured in light years.*

VOCABULARY

asterism—*a group of stars in a larger constellation*

constellation—*a pattern formed by stars in the sky*

light year—*the distance light can travel in a year (about 6 trillion miles)*

Identifying Constellations

Study the constellations illustrated on this page. Take the page home tonight and see which ones you can identify in the night sky. Some, but not all, of the constellations will be visible. Different constellations are visible at different parts of the year.

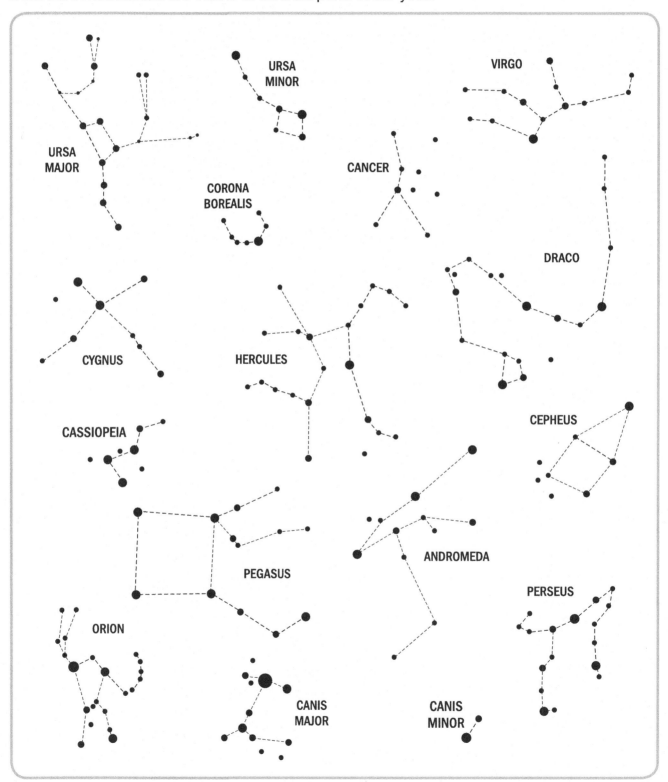

Hanging Constellations

Materials
- *wire clothes hanger*
- *small, colored star stickers*
- *blue plastic wrap*
- *black marker*
- *clear tape*

Directions

1. Choose one constellation from those illustrated on page 52.

2. Bend the wire clothes hanger so that it forms a rectangle or parallelogram.

3. Cut a piece of blue plastic wrap large enough to fit around both sides of the hanger.

4. Carefully flatten and wrap the blue plastic wrap around both faces of the hanger. Tightly smooth the blue plastic to the wire edges of the hanger. Use clear tape to tighten the wrap if the plastic wrap won't stick to the wire.

5. Arrange the shiny stars in the same formation as the constellation you chose. Firmly stick the colored star stickers to the plastic wrap.

6. Use a black marker to outline the pattern of the stars and label the constellation.

7. Display the constellation on a bulletin board or in a window.

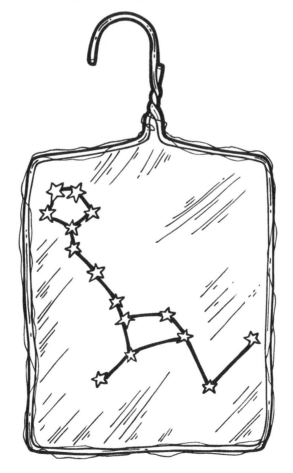

Student Inquiry Activity

Choose one of the constellations pictured below as the focus of your inquiry investigation. (*Note:* This project may take several weeks.) Make sure that it is visible in the night sky at the time of year you are doing this investigation.

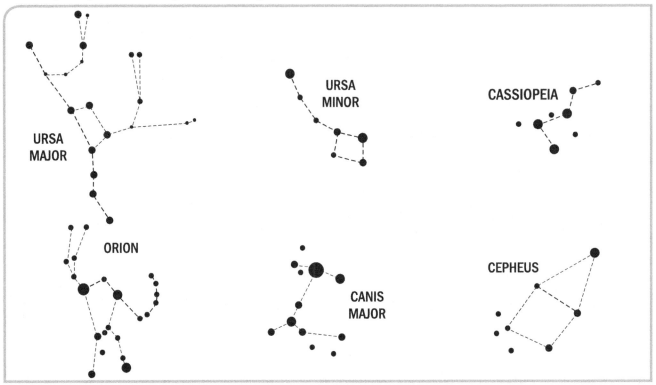

Which constellation did you choose? _____

Why did you pick that constellation? _____

Choose either of these two investigation opportunities.

1. Observe the changes in the constellation's location and direction in the night sky each night for two to four weeks.

2. Observe the changes in the constellation's location and direction in the night sky over a period of several hours with its position noted for each hour.

Making Predictions

What do you think will happen to the constellation's location? Sketch the location and direction you might expect at two different times.

N

Date: _____

Time: _____   W   E

Date: _____

Time: _____

S

Do the Investigation

Carefully map the location and direction of your constellation in the night sky on separate papers. Record the date and time. Report the results to your class.

The Moon

DID YOU KNOW THAT . . . ?

- *The near side of the moon always faces Earth. The far side never faces Earth.*

- *The gravitational pull of the moon creates two daily tides on Earth's oceans.*

- *An astronaut's footprint on the moon may last for 100 million years.*

- *The moon and Earth are both about 4.6 billion years old.*

PHYSICAL FEATURES

The moon and Earth were formed at the same time, about 4.6 billion years ago. They differ greatly, however, in many important ways. Although they travel together in a yearly voyage around the Sun, the moon is also always in motion around Earth. The length of that orbit is 27.3 days, about a month. The original concept of the month developed in several cultures from the regular movement of the moon.

THE MOON'S SURFACE

Unlike Earth, the moon has a very low gravitational pull and has no atmosphere. No air or gasses of any kind cover the moon as they do over Earth. The surface gravity of the moon is only 16% of Earth's, so water and gases would not be held by the moon's gravity. This lack of water or an atmosphere results in a surface that has changed very little over millions of years. Dust and rocks thrown up by meteors stay in the same location for long periods of time because there are no forces of weathering and erosion constantly changing the surface.

When early astronomers observed a full moon, they thought the dark areas looked like seas. They are still called seas today although we now know that they were huge lava flows resulting from cracks in the moon's crust and volcanoes that existed early in its history. Some "seas" or basins were created by meteorites smashing into the moon. There are more meteor craters on the far side of the moon than on the side facing Earth. The moon also has mountains, one of which is almost as high as Mount Everest, the highest mountain on Earth.

The moon is about one-fourth the size of Earth. It has a diameter (distance across) of 2,160 miles, about the distance from Los Angeles to Chicago. The average distance of the moon from Earth is 238,900 miles. Because the moon lacks any atmosphere, the temperature can rise to over 260°F, which is hotter than boiling water. It can be as cold as −280°F, which is colder than any place on Earth.

The Moon

PHASES OF THE MOON

As the moon orbits Earth, half its surface is lit by the Sun, while the other half remains in darkness. The phases of the moon reflect the changes in the moon's shape as it faces Earth, when different sections of its surface facing Earth are lighted by the Sun's light.

When the moon is between the Sun and Earth, its lighted side faces away from Earth and the side facing Earth is dark. This is the new moon phase. As the moon continues its orbit, more of the lighted portion becomes visible from Earth. A small, lighted **crescent** or sliver becomes visible after a new moon. This sliver grows larger each night and is called a "**waxing**" crescent. It grows each night until the first quarter is visible. At this point, half of the lighted part of the moon is visible from Earth.

As the lighted portion continues to expand, it becomes known as the "waxing" **gibbous** phase. Gibbous means "humped" and the light is swelling over the moon until a full moon occurs about two weeks after the new moon. At this point, the entire lighted side of the moon is visible to Earth. Gradually, the moon enters the **"waning"** or declining gibbous phase where the lighted portion is less and less visible. In the last quarter, half of the lighted portion of the moon is visible. In the waning crescent, less visible light is seen each night. The moon then enters another new moon phase and the cycle repeats itself. Because the lunar schedule is not a full 30 days, some years have 12 full moons and others have 13 full moons. The boundary between the light and dark portions of the lunar surface is called the **terminator**.

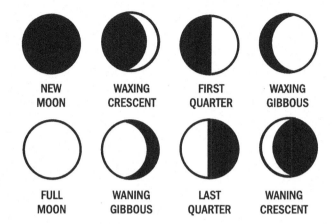

| NEW MOON | WAXING CRESCENT | FIRST QUARTER | WAXING GIBBOUS |
| FULL MOON | WANING GIBBOUS | LAST QUARTER | WANING CRESCENT |

ECLIPSES OF THE MOON

Eclipses are caused by the alignment of the Sun, the moon, and Earth. A lunar eclipse occurs when the moon passes into Earth's shadow. Lunar eclipses occur only when there is a full moon and Earth is between the Sun and the moon. At most full moons, the moon is above or below Earth's shadow. From two to five times a year, the full moon does pass through Earth's shadow creating an eclipse of some kind.

Facts to Remember

- *The moon goes through the same phases every month.*
- *The same side of the moon always faces Earth.*

VOCABULARY

crescent—*a sliver of visible light on the moon*

eclipse—*blocking sight of the moon or Sun*

gibbous—*humped or swelling*

terminator—*the boundary between the light and dark part of the moon*

waning—*getting smaller*

waxing—*getting larger*

Moon Chart

Directions: Start this moon chart when the moon is full. Try to record the information at the same time every night.

Day 1   **Sketch**

Date: _____

Time: _____

Weather Conditions: _____

Direction of the Moon: North   East   South   West

Phase of the Moon: _____

Day 2   **Sketch**

Date: _____

Time: _____

Weather Conditions: _____

Direction of the Moon: North   East   South   West

Phase of the Moon: _____

Day 3   **Sketch**

Date: _____

Time: _____

Weather Conditions: _____

Direction of the Moon: North   East   South   West

Phase of the Moon: _____

Day 4   **Sketch**

Date: _____

Time: _____

Weather Conditions: _____

Direction of the Moon: North   East   South   West

Phase of the Moon: _____

Day 5   **Sketch**

Date: _____

Time: _____

Weather Conditions: _____

Direction of the Moon: North   East   South   West

Phase of the Moon: _____

Phases of the Moon

Directions: Record the dates for each phase of the moon for a 30-day period.

New Moon

Date: _____
Date: _____
Date: _____
Date: _____

Waxing Crescent

Date: _____
Date: _____
Date: _____
Date: _____

First Quarter

Date: _____
Date: _____
Date: _____
Date: _____

Waxing Gibbous

Date: _____
Date: _____
Date: _____
Date: _____

Full Moon

Date: _____
Date: _____
Date: _____
Date: _____

Waning Gibbous

Date: _____
Date: _____
Date: _____
Date: _____

Last Quarter

Date: _____
Date: _____
Date: _____
Date: _____

Waning Crescent

Date: _____
Date: _____
Date: _____
Date: _____

Student Inquiry Activity

This page will help you get your inquiry activity started. This project may take 30 days.

Inquiry Questions

Isaac Newton said that he got headaches trying to understand all of the complicated movements of the moon. Consider these inquiry questions about the moon.

- Where is the moon located in the night sky at 7:00 PM, 8:00 PM, or at any specific time in the night?
- When is the moon visible in the morning?
- Where is the moon located in the morning sky when it is visible?
- How long does it take for the moon to cross the night sky?
- How does the moon's location change during the night?
- Does the moon always move in the same direction?

Write some inquiry questions of your own about the moon.

1. _____
2. _____
3. _____

Getting Started

1. Choose one inquiry question to investigate.

2. State your hypothesis. What do you think is the answer?

3. Briefly explain how and when the hypothesis might be tested by observation of the moon.

4. Draw a sketch indicating what you think is the answer to the question. The sketch will illustrate your hypothesis.

Inquiry Question: _____

_____

My Hypothesis: I think that . . . _____

_____

How would the hypothesis be tested by observation? _____

_____

Sketch

Do the Investigation

Use the Student Inquiry Worksheets to complete your assignment. You may wish to change inquiry questions before you start. Carefully map the location and direction of the moon on the worksheet as part of your investigation. Report the results to your class.

The Solar System

DID YOU KNOW THAT . . . ?

- *The Sun is almost 25 trillion miles from the next nearest star.*

- *The temperature at the center of the Sun is almost 27 million degrees Fahrenheit.*

- *The Sun will expand and die 5 billion years from now.*

- *The gravitational pull of the Sun has a range of more than three-and-a-half billion miles.*

Our solar system is dominated by the Sun. It is a globe of burning gas, primarily hydrogen, which provides the energy that heats and lights planets. The Sun exerts a gravitational pull, which keeps the planets rotating in regular orbits around the Sun. The four inner planets have rocky surfaces and are relatively small. The four outer planets and one dwarf planet include four very large gas giants. They are gigantic balls of liquids and gases held together by gravity. The dwarf planet, Pluto, is covered with rock and ice. Most asteroids are rocky, metallic chunks of many different sizes that orbit the Sun in a belt between Mars and Jupiter. Many planets have orbiting moons. Comets are huge ice lumps that travel through space and occasionally come near the Sun.

THE INNER PLANETS

Mercury
Diameter: 3,029 miles
Distance from the Sun:
 36,000,000 miles
Length of Year: 88 days
Length of Day: 59 Earth days
Highest Temperature: 810°F
Number of Moons: 0
Interesting Fact: Mercury has the fastest orbiting
 speed around the Sun.

Venus
Diameter: 7,521 miles
Distance from the Sun:
 67,200,000 miles
Length of Year: 225 days
Length of Day: 243 Earth days
Highest Temperature: 867°F
Number of Moons: 0
Interesting Fact: Venus has the hottest temperatures
 of any planet.

Earth
Diameter: 7,926 miles
Distance from the Sun:
 93,000,000 miles
Length of Year: 365 days
Length of Day: 1 day (24 hours)
Highest Temperature: 133°F
Number of Moons: 1
Interesting Fact: Earth is the only known planet to
 support life.

Mars
Diameter: 4,221 miles
Distance from the Sun:
 141,500,000 miles
Length of Year: 687 days
Length of Day: 24.5 hours
Highest Temperature: 77°F
Number of Moons: 2
Interesting Fact: Mars is called the red planet.

The Solar System

OUTER PLANETS

Jupiter
Diameter: 88,846 miles
Distance from the Sun: 483,300,000 miles
Length of Year: 11.9 years
Length of Day: 10 hours
Highest Temperature: −238°F
Number of Moons: at least 63
Interesting Fact: Jupiter is so large it could hold 1,300 Earths.

Saturn
Diameter: 74,898 miles
Distance from the Sun: 886,700,000 miles
Length of Year: 29.5 years
Length of Day: 10.6 hours
Highest Temperature: −292°F
Number of Moons: at least 47
Interesting Fact: Saturn is so light that it would float on a lake.

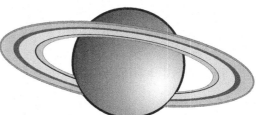

Uranus
Diameter: 31,763 miles
Distance from the Sun: 1,782,000,000 miles
Length of Year: 84 years
Length of Day: 17 hours
Highest Temperature: −353°F
Number of Moons: at least 27
Interesting Fact: Uranus spins on its side.

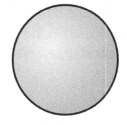

Neptune
Diameter: 30,775 miles
Distance from the Sun: 2,774,000,000 miles
Length of Year: 164.9 years
Length of Day: 16 hours
Highest Temperature: −364°F
Number of Moons: at least 13
Interesting Fact: Neptune has the fastest winds in the solar system.

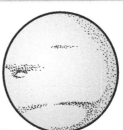

Pluto (dwarf planet)
Diameter: 1,432 miles
Distance from the Sun: 3,672,000,000 miles
Length of Year: 248.6 years
Length of Day: 6.4 days
Highest Temperature: −382°F
Number of Moons: 1
Interesting Fact: Pluto was reclassified as a dwarf planet after a vote by astronomers on August 24, 2006.

The Planets

Directions: Use the planet information on pages 60 and 61 to answer these questions.

1. Which planet is farthest from the Sun? _____

2. Which planet has the biggest diameter (distance across)? _____

3. Which planet has the most moons? _____

4. Which two planets have no moons? _____   _____

5. Which planet has the highest temperature? _____

6. Which planet has the longest year? _____

7. Which planet has the shortest year? _____

8. Which planet has the longest day? _____

9. Which planet has the shortest day? _____

10. Which planet has the smallest diameter (distance across)? _____

Assignment

Design a bulletin board display for one planet. Cut a large sheet of white paper into a big circle. Color the circle with the appropriate colors for the planet. List all the facts you can find about the planet. Use pages 60 and 61 as well as other sources for more detailed information. Other facts you might find in addition to the planet's color might be its mass, density, orbital speed as it travels around the Sun, and gravitational pull. Write your details, ideas, or plan on the lines below.

_____

_____

_____

_____

_____

_____

_____

_____

_____

_____

_____

_____

_____

_____

Comparing the Size of Planets

Materials
- *butcher paper*
- *metric ruler*
- *meter stick (if available)*
- *compass (for making circles)*
- *string*
- *tape*

Directions

On the chart below, round the diameter of each planet to the nearest thousand miles. Use pages 60 and 61 to complete the chart. Drop the last three zeroes from the rounded number to find the centimeter scale.

Planet	Actual Diameter	Rounded Diameter	Centimeter Scale
Mercury	3,029 miles	3,000 miles	3 cm
Venus	7,521 miles	8,000 miles	8 cm
Earth	_____	_____	_____
Mars	_____	_____	_____
Jupiter	_____	_____	89 cm
Saturn	_____	_____	_____
Uranus	_____	_____	_____
Neptune	_____	_____	_____
Pluto (dwarf)	_____	_____	_____

Directions

You may complete this project with a partner. (Using a compass is helpful.)

1. Carefully cut out a paper circle with a diameter (distance across the circle in any direction) of 3 cm. Label it "Mercury."
2. Cut out a circle with a diameter of 8 cm. Label it "Venus."
3. Use the same procedure for each of the remaining planets. Be sure to use the centimeter scale. You will need a meter stick or several rulers for the larger numbers.
4. Display your planets on a bulletin board with the smallest on top and the largest on the bottom.

Making Large Round Circles

You can use this trick for making large, round circles on big pieces of butcher paper. (*Note:* You can also use a compass to draw a circle.)

1. Measure a piece of string the length of the centimeter scale—for 89 centimeters, for example.
2. Tape or hold both ends of the string on one pencil in the center of the paper where you want to draw a circle.
3. Tape or hold a second pencil in the loop made by the string.
4. Keep the string tight and draw the circle around the paper.

Student Inquiry Activity

This page will help you get your inquiry activity started.

Thinking About the Solar System

- What planets can you see in the night sky?
- Where are the planets in the night sky located?
- How can you tell planets from stars?
- What would life be like as an astronaut on Mars?
- How long would it take a space shuttle to travel to each planet?
- Where is the Sun located at each hour of the day in the sky?

What Would You Like to Know About the Sun and the Planets?

1. _____
2. _____
3. _____

Planning an Inquiry Investigation

Which of the questions on this page could be tested with an inquiry investigation using observation and recording data?

Possible Inquiry Investigation: _____

_____

Possible Inquiry Investigation: _____

_____

Getting Started

Choose one inquiry question. Then write a hypothesis for this question. Write a possible step-by-step plan for completing this investigation.

Inquiry Question: _____

_____

Hypothesis: I think that . . . _____

_____

Step 1: _____

_____

Step 2: _____

_____

Step 3: _____

_____

Doing the Science Inquiry

Use the Student Inquiry Worksheets to complete your planning and to do the inquiry investigation.

Clouds

DID YOU KNOW THAT . . . ?

- *About 500 million tons of water go through the water cycle every year.*

- *There may be as many as 44,000 storms a day over the earth.*

WATER CYCLE

Nature cleans the water you use in a natural cycle. The elements of the water you drink have been used billions of times before for hundreds of millions of years by plants and animals, from bacteria to dinosaurs to house pets. The system is remarkably effective and crucial to life. Because water is the essential compound used by all living things, it is important that all living things have access to water in some form.

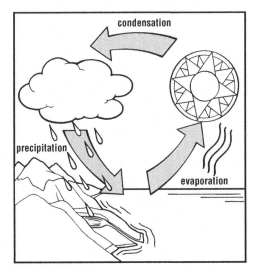

EVAPORATION

Water evaporates from oceans, rivers, and lakes due to the heat of the Sun. The water vapor that evaporates is in the form of a gas. The process of **evaporation** separates the water from any impurities, such as dirt, waste products, salt, germs, and soap. This is a natural process of purification.

CONDENSATION

Warm air can hold more water vapor than cool air. As the water vapor rises, it cools and the air becomes saturated or filled with water vapor and forms clouds. If the saturated air keeps rising and cools even more, water vapor condenses into drops of liquid water— this is called **condensation**. The rising air and clouds often move over land areas.

PRECIPITATION

When the droplets of water in a cloud move around, they push into each other and grow larger. When the droplets of water in clouds become too heavy, they fall as rain, snow, or hail. This is called **precipitation**. When the rain or snow falls on land, some of it is used or absorbed by the soil. Some is used by plants and animals. Some is released as water vapor. All of the water eventually flows back in rivers, lakes, and oceans where the process is repeated.

CLOUD TYPES

There are three basic types of clouds: cumulus, stratus, and cirrus. All other cloud names represent variations in terms of shape and location. These clouds are formed by the water cycle. They hold the water as vapor and liquid droplets until it falls as precipitation.

Unit 10

Clouds

CUMULUS CLOUDS

Cumulus clouds look like heaps of white mashed potatoes or giant cotton balls. They form in the sunny sky in warm weather. As the water evaporates into this type of cloud, the warm air rises, it forms into a round mass, and it spreads out. The cooler air causes some of the water vapor to condense into liquid droplets forming a visible cloud. Cumulus clouds usually form below 6,000 feet, which is a little more than a mile. They don't usually form rain but in certain conditions can form thunderclouds.

STRATUS CLOUDS

Stratus clouds are spread out. They usually form between a layer of warm damp air moving over a layer of cool air. These low-lying clouds often create fog, which is basically a cloud at ground level. Stratus clouds form low, flat layers of dark clouds. They usually block out the sunshine.

CIRRUS CLOUDS

Cirrus clouds look like thin, wispy locks of white hair. They form very high in the sky at 20,000 feet or more. They are formed by ice crystals instead of liquid water. These crystals are so thin that sunlight shines through them. Cirrus clouds are often visible high in the sky when the weather is good. They look like thin trails or streaks of clouds.

RAIN AND SNOW

When a cloud name is combined with **nimbus**, that cloud will bring precipitation. Nimbostratus clouds are thick, dark clouds with many layers lying close to the ground. They bring a lot of rain or snow. Huge, billowing cumulonimbus clouds several miles high can bring heavy rain, thunderstorms, or tornadoes.

Facts to Remember

- *The water cycle purifies water and constantly resupplies water to the land.*

- *The three main types of clouds are cumulus, stratus, and cirrus.*

- *Nimbostratus are thick, dark, low clouds which bring rain.*

- *Water is cleaned through the process of evaporation.*

VOCABULARY

cirrus—*high, thin, white, streaky clouds*

condensation—*to cool water vapor into liquid drops*

cumulus—*puffy, white clouds*

evaporation—*to turn liquid water into water vapor, a gas*

nimbus—*dark, rain-bearing cloud*

precipitation—*rain, snow, or hail*

stratus—*low, foggy clouds*

Making a Cloud

Materials
- *clear drinking glass*
- *match or chalk dust*
- *small, resealable plastic bag*
- *ice cubes*
- *flashlight*
- *jar lid or small saucer*
- *hot water*

Directions

1. Fill the drinking glass with hot water.

2. Place a bag with four or five ice cubes in a jar lid or small plastic saucer on top of the glass. It should fit firmly on the top of the glass and allow no heat to escape.

3. Ask a teacher or adult to light a match and let it burn for a moment in the air above the hot water. Immediately replace the ice and lid. Use some chalk dust if matches are not available.

4. Position everyone in a circle around the glass at eye level.

5. Turn off all lights except the flashlight.

6. Shine the flashlight through the glass.

7. Observe the swirling clouds above the water.

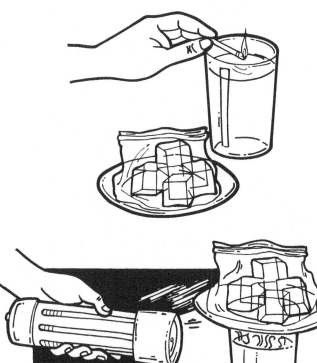

What Happened

The steam rising from the hot water condensed into droplets of water when it met the cold air cooled by the ice cubes. The droplets attached themselves to the particles of smoke or dust just as water vapor in a cloud is attached to dust, smoke, salt, and other particles in the air.

Try It Again

Do the same experiment again, but try changing one or two factors. Use cooler water, less smoke, fewer ice cubes, or some other element. Observe the results.

Identifying Clouds

Note: Complete this activity on a day with many clouds in the sky.

Cumulus

Cirrus

Stratus

Nimbostratus

Directions

1. Study the clouds illustrated above.
2. Face north and sketch the clouds visible in that direction. Label the clouds with your best guess.
3. Follow the same procedure for east, south, and west. Use the back of this page if you need more room.
4. Share your observations with the class.

North

West   **East**

South

Student Inquiry Activity

You will want to do this activity with cloudy weather. This page will help you get your inquiry activity started.

Questions About Clouds

Go outside with this paper. Look up in the sky and watch the clouds. Let your mind roam free with the clouds. Write down any questions that you would like to answer about clouds.

1. _____
2. _____
3. _____
4. _____

Inquiry Suggestions

Read these inquiry investigation questions.

- Do dark clouds always mean that rain will come soon?
- Does the size of clouds indicate how much rain will fall in your community?
- Which clouds are in the sky before rainfall?
- Which clouds are in the sky before snowfall?

Starting Your Inquiry Investigation

Choose your inquiry question. Then write your hypothesis. Write a planning guide for doing this investigation.

Inquiry Investigation Question: _____

_____

Your Hypothesis: I think that . . . _____

_____

First Step: _____

_____

Second Step: _____

_____

Third Step: _____

_____

Completing the Investigation

Use the Student Inquiry Worksheets to record your observations and draw your conclusions from this inquiry.

Weather

DID YOU KNOW THAT . . . ?

- *In 1999, a tornado in Oklahoma had a wind speed of 318 miles per hour, about five times as fast as a car driving on a freeway.*

- *Vostok, Antarctica recorded a temperature of –132°F in 1983. This is 164 degrees below freezing.*

- *Yuma, Arizona has over 4,000 hours of bright sunshine each year, an average of almost 11 hours every day.*

- *The hottest temperature on Earth, 133°F, was recorded in the El Azizia Desert in Libya in 1922.*

WHAT IS WEATHER?

Weather is the general term for the behavior of Earth's atmosphere and its daily changes. There are three main features of weather. They are temperature, air movement, and the amount of water vapor in the air. Other aspects of weather include sunshine, precipitation, cloud formations, the direction and force of winds, and atmospheric pressure.

CLIMATE

The average weather in an area over a long period of time, 50 to 100 years, is called **climate**. Climates are named for their location or certain prevailing conditions. Climates may still have a wide variety of weather patterns depending on the time of the year and conditions throughout the world. Polar climates usually feature cold temperatures, short summers, and limited snowfall. Mountain climates are cooler and often have more precipitation than lower altitudes. Desert climates are usually dry and either hot or cold. Tropical climates are hot and rainy. Temperate climates feature warm summers, cool winters, and moderate precipitation year round.

SUNSHINE

The most important factor in the weather is the Sun. It provides heat for our planet. The heat created by the Sun leads to the evaporation of water, cloud formation, rain and snow, and wind.

WIND

When the Sun heats Earth, the air gets hotter. This causes the air to expand, get lighter, and rise. To replace the rising hot air and fill the area of low pressure caused by the rising air, a mass of colder, denser, heavier air pushes down into the empty space. This constant circulation of air creates wind. Because air seldom stops moving, it carries heat and water around the world.

Weather

CLOUDS

Clouds are created as a part of the water cycle by the evaporation of water from the surfaces of oceans, lakes, and rivers. Clouds are good indicators of weather. Dark, low-lying nimbostratus clouds blocking the Sun usually bring rain or snow. Puffy, white clouds suggest warm weather and sunshine. High, wispy cirrus clouds indicate that rain may be coming soon.

PRECIPITATION

Precipitation is the name for water that falls to Earth's surface from clouds. Rain may vary from light drizzle, which barely wets the surface, to drenching rains lasting days. In freezing temperatures, the form of precipitation is snow. Sleet is a mixture of snow and drizzle.

TEMPERATURE

Temperature is the degree of hotness or coldness of the air close to Earth's surface. Temperatures are highest near the Equator where the Sun's rays meet Earth on a direct line, and there are few clouds to block the direct heat of the Sun. Temperatures are colder at the poles because the Sun's rays

reach the poles on an angle. Temperatures in temperate areas are usually cooler at night and warmer during the day, and extreme temperatures are rare.

AIR PRESSURE

Air pressure is the force of gravity pulling air toward Earth. The pressure is greatest at ground level because the weight of all the air above is greater than it is higher in the atmosphere. Air pressure varies and strongly affects weather. Air pressure is measured with a barometer.

STORMS AND EXTREME WEATHER

Special combinations of weather factors may create violent storms and extreme weather conditions. These can be thunder and lightning storms, hurricanes, tornadoes, blizzards, and droughts.

Facts to Remember

● *Three main components of weather are temperature, precipitation, and wind.*

VOCABULARY

air pressure—*the weight or gravitational pull of the air*

climate—*weather in a region over a long period of time*

precipitation—*rain and snow*

temperature—*the hotness or coldness of the air*

Daily Weather Log

Directions: Record the information about your home or school on the log. Be as accurate as you can. Compare your results with the nightly weather report on the television news report.

Day 1
Temperature when school begins: _____
Temperature at noon: _____
Temperature when school ends: _____
Precipitation (light showers, steady rain, thunder showers, heavy snowfall): _____
_____
Wind (breezy, gusts, heavy, occasional): _____
Clouds (describe): _____
Other information: _____

Day 2
Temperature when school begins: _____
Temperature at noon: _____
Temperature when school ends: _____
Precipitation (light showers, steady rain, thunder showers, heavy snowfall): _____
_____
Wind (breezy, gusts, heavy, occasional): _____
Clouds (describe): _____
Other information: _____

Day 3
Temperature when school begins: _____
Temperature at noon: _____
Temperature when school ends: _____
Precipitation (light showers, steady rain, thunder showers, heavy snowfall): _____
_____
Wind (breezy, gusts, heavy, occasional): _____
Clouds (describe): _____
Other information: _____

Day 4
Temperature when school begins: _____
Temperature at noon: _____
Temperature when school ends: _____
Precipitation (light showers, steady rain, thunder showers, heavy snowfall): _____
_____
Wind (breezy, gusts, heavy, occasional): _____
Clouds (describe): _____
Other information: _____

Making a Model Thermometer

Materials
- *clear, plastic water bottle*
- *clear, plastic packing tape*
- *small index cards or pieces of tagboard*
- *modeling clay*
- *food coloring*
- *marker*
- *straws*

Directions

1. Clear any labels off a clear, plastic water bottle.

2. Fill the bottle half full of water. Mark the water line with a colored marker.

3. Put two or three drops of dark food coloring in the water.

4. Make a centimeter gauge as shown along the page. Start with a line at zero and number from zero to 15 going up the scale from bottom to top.

5. Use clear, plastic packing tape to fasten the gauge on the bottle with the zero line at the bottom, even with the waterline.

6. Set the straw in the bottle so that one end is an inch or more into the water and the other end above the bottle.

7. Surround the straw with one ounce of modeling clay by carefully molding the clay around the straw at the mouth of the bottle so that air can only escape though the straw. This is very important.

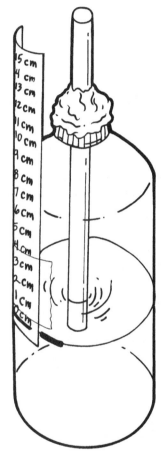

15 cm
14 cm
13 cm
12 cm
11 cm
10 cm
9 cm
8 cm
7 cm
6 cm
5 cm
4 cm
3 cm
2 cm
1 cm
0 cm

Using the Model Thermometer

Place the model thermometer in a warm or hot location. If it works correctly, water will rise up and may spill out of the straw. The gauge tells how far the water rose. If it doesn't work, check the clay seal on the mouth of the bottle.

Why It Works

The Sun heats the air in the bottle. This causes the air to expand and push down on the water. Pushing down on the water causes the water to rise up the straw. The hotter the air becomes, the greater the pressure on the water, and the higher the water rises in the straw.

Student Inquiry Activity

This page will help you get your inquiry activity started. Use the Student Inquiry Worksheets for a guideline as you complete this inquiry activity.

Weather Questions

- Can you predict tomorrow's weather—temperature, precipitation, and wind—based on today's indicators?

- Can you predict next week's weather based on indicators this week for temperature, wind, and precipitation (rain and snow)?

- How does the location of your community affect the weather in your community? Does the presence of a lake, ocean, mountain, or grassland affect your weather pattern?

- Can you make a weather map showing a predictable pattern of weather—temperature, wind, and precipitation (rain and snow)—for a week, a month, or a year?

- How much does the daily forecast for the weather in your neighborhood vary from the actual weather you get at your home or school?

- How accurate is the weekly weather forecast on your television, on the Internet, or in the newspaper? How different is the weather at your school or home from the prediction?

Brainstorming

How would you go about investigating any of the questions listed above?

Inquiry Question: _____

_____

How You Would Do the Investigation: _____

_____

_____

Inquiry Question: _____

_____

How You Would Do the Investigation: _____

_____

_____

Consulting Classmates

Meet with a classmate. Then share your brainstorming ideas. Share other ideas for inquiry questions.

Becoming Weather Testers

Use the Student Inquiry Worksheets to plan your inquiry investigation and record your data.

States of Matter

DID YOU KNOW THAT . . . ?

- *Plasma is a fourth state of matter that forms when molecules become so hot that electrons become separated from their atoms.*

- *It takes billions of molecules of air to fill a balloon. Each of these molecules can travel as fast as a jet airplane.*

- *Carbon dioxide can change from a solid block of dry ice to a gas and back again without becoming a liquid.*

- *A million atoms could fit on the period at the end of this sentence.*

Matter is the name given to all of the material in the universe. It makes up suns and planets, soil and water, and rocks and air. Matter is made up of particles called **atoms**. Atoms can be arranged in the form of solids, liquids, and gases. At extremely high temperatures, such as that produced by the Sun and other stars, a fourth state of matter called *plasma* is formed.

SOLIDS

The molecules in solids are strongly attracted to each other. They are closely connected in tight bonds and don't move around very much. Solids retain the same size and shape in a defined structure. The only movement of the molecules occurs when they vibrate when a solid is struck. Wooden boards, books, rocks, and hammers are examples of solids.

LIQUIDS

The molecules that form liquids are not as tightly arranged. They are not as strongly attracted to each other and have greater energy, but there is a limited, exact volume. Liquid molecules can move around more. Liquids take the shape of whatever container they are in. Oil, water, alcohol, and blood are liquids. High temperatures can often convert solids into liquids. Even rocks and metal objects can become liquids.

GASES

The molecules in gases are barely attracted to each other. The molecules are very loosely connected. These molecules have a lot of energy and are free to move in all directions. They have no shape of their own. They take the shape of whatever container they are in. The molecules spread out throughout the container that holds them. Gases include water vapor, carbon dioxide, helium, and air.

States of Matter

WATER MOLECULES

Water easily moves from one state of matter to another. If the temperature is below 32°F, liquid water will freeze into ice. Ice forms solid blocks with clearly defined shapes. Water is a liquid at temperatures between 32°F and 212°F. It takes the shape of whatever container it is in, although the same amount of water will look different in containers that are not alike. Water becomes steam or water vapor at temperatures above 212°F. The gas molecules move very fast, spread out into whatever space is available, and have no shape of their own.

FREEZING AND MELTING

A liquid becomes a solid when it is cooled to a certain temperature. This temperature varies for each kind of matter. The **freezing point** and the **melting point** of most substances are the same. The freezing point of pure water is 32°F, but water with impurities requires a colder temperature. The freezing point of iron is 2,802°F. The freezing (or melting) point of wax is 137°F. The melting point for gold is 1,947°F.

EVAPORATION AND CONDENSATION

Evaporation and **condensation** occur at the **boiling point** of a liquid. Water boils at 212°F, and the liquid becomes water vapor. When the water vapor is cooled, it condenses and returns to a liquid form.

Evaporation of water also occurs in nature at lower temperatures when the heat energy of the Sun causes the water molecules at the surface of a body of water to vibrate and escape into the air. Wind also increases this vibration and speeds up the process of evaporation. If the humidity is high, the air is already full of water vapor, and evaporation is slower. This is why sweat evaporates slowly on humid days when the air is filled with water vapor.

Facts to Remember

- *There are three states of matter: solids, liquids, and gases.*

- *Solids do not change shapes.*

- *Liquids have the save volume but are shaped by their container.*

- *Gases have no fixed shape or volume.*

- *Water is commonly seen in all three forms: solid, liquid, and gas.*

- *Water is evaporated by energy from the Sun and wind.*

VOCABULARY

atom—*a tiny unit of matter*

boiling point—*the point at which a liquid becomes a gas*

condensation—*changing a gas to a liquid*

evaporation—*changing a liquid to a gas*

freezing point (melting point)—*the point at which a liquid becomes a solid or a solid melts into a liquid*

matter—*the material in the universe*

Observing Evaporation

Materials
- *sand or soil*
- *cups*
- *plastic teaspoon*
- *food coloring*
- *plastic-coated plate*
- *water*
- *salt*
- *rocks*

Directions

Complete this project on a warm, somewhat breezy day. Start in the morning.

1. Pour three ounces of water into a cup. Mark the water level.
2. Add a few drops of food coloring to the water and stir.
3. Stir in a teaspoon of salt with the water.
4. Stir in a teaspoon of sand or soil.
5. Place a plastic-coated plate on a table in the sun. Use a fist-sized rock to hold the plate in place.
6. Carefully pour the cup of water onto the plate.
7. Observe and record results hourly throughout the day.

Evaporation Record Form

First Observation

What changes can you see? _____

_____

How can you tell if the water is evaporating? _____

_____

Second Observation

What changes can you see? _____

_____

How can you tell if the water is evaporating? _____

_____

Third Observation

What changes can you see? _____

_____

How can you tell if the water is evaporating? _____

_____

Final Observation

What changes can you see? _____

_____

How can you tell if the water is evaporating? _____

_____

Pour the water back into the cup. Mark the water level. How much of the water evaporated?

_____

More Observing Evaporation

Materials
- *ice cubes*
- *one-ounce (30 mm) cups*
- *clear, plastic cup*
- *empty, clear water bottle with cap*
- *marker*
- *water*

How Much Water Is in an Ice Cube?

Complete this project on a warm day. Start in the morning.

1. Place one ice cube in a plastic cup in the classroom where it can melt but not much evaporation can occur.
2. Check on the ice cube regularly.
3. Use the one-ounce cup to measure the amount of liquid produced from the ice cube.
4. Record your results on this observation form.

Observation Form

Time started: _____

Time the ice finished melting: _____

Number of minutes it took to melt: _____

Amount of liquid water produced: _____

Observing Evaporation in a Closed System

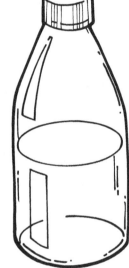

1. Pour tap water in a clear, empty water bottle until it is half full.
2. Mark the waterline with a colored marker on the outside of the bottle.
3. Put the cap on the bottle and set it outside in a warm location.
4. Observe the bottle on an hourly basis.
5. Complete the observation form below.

First Observation

Has any condensation occurred on the upper half of the bottle? What does it look like?

_____

_____

Has the water gotten lower than the waterline you marked? Why?

_____

Second Observation

Has any condensation occurred on the upper half of the bottle? What does it look like?

_____

_____

Has the water gotten lower than the waterline you marked? Why?

_____

Final Observation

Describe what happened. _____

_____

Student Inquiry Activity

This activity can be done alone or by a team of two students. This page will help you get your inquiry activity started.

Thinking About Solids, Liquids, and Gases

List as many solids, liquids, and gases as you can think of.   Use elements or compound names. Some examples are listed.

Solid	Liquid	Gas
ice	water	water vapor
iron	oil	oxygen
salt	soap	carbon dioxide
_____	_____	_____
_____	_____	_____
_____	_____	_____
_____	_____	_____

What Do You Think?

- How could you make oil into a solid?
- How could you make liquid soap into a solid?
- How does evaporation separate solids and liquids?
- How can you make water into a solid?
- Will oil evaporate?
- What common household liquids will not evaporate?

Thinking It Out

1. Which of the inquiry questions above would you like to try to investigate? _____
   _____

2. What is your hypothesis? _____
   _____

3. What could you do to answer the question and test the hypothesis? _____
   _____

4. What materials would you need? _____
   _____

5. What help would you need? _____
   _____

Following A Plan

Use the Student Inquiry Worksheets to make your final choice, plan your investigation, record your results, and draw conclusions.

Light

DID YOU KNOW THAT . . . ?

- *All warm objects give off infrared rays.*

- *Ultraviolet rays are responsible for sunburns and tans.*

- *Every object in the universe gives off electromagnetic waves—suns, trees, plants, and even humans.*

NATURE OF LIGHT

For more than two hundred years, brilliant scientists debated whether light was a kind of wave or whether it was made up of very tiny particles of one kind or another. Discoveries in the twentieth century (January 1, 1901– December 31, 2000) by Albert Einstein and other scientists led to the idea of light being composed of very tiny packages of energy called **photons**. These photons can at times behave like particles and at other times act like waves, but they are never particles and waves at the same time. The idea of photons helped scientists understand how light could travel through the vacuum of space and how it could travel in straight rays and create clear shadows.

ELECTROMAGNETIC RADIATION

The visible light we see is one part of a very large range of electromagnetic radiation in the universe. It is the only part of the electromagnetic spectrum that we can see. Other forms of electromagnetic radiation are radio waves, television waves, radar waves, microwaves, infrared rays, ultraviolet rays, x-rays, gamma rays, and cosmic rays. Many of these forms of electromagnetic radiation are of great use to humans.

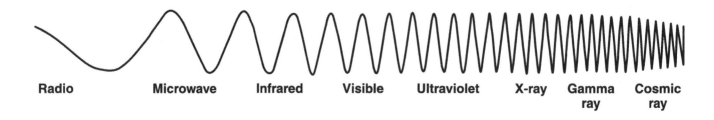

Radio   Microwave   Infrared   Visible   Ultraviolet   X-ray   Gamma ray   Cosmic ray

Light

TRANSPARENT, TRANSLUCENT, AND OPAQUE OBJECTS

Rays of light travel in a straight line. They may pass through an object, bounce off, or be absorbed. Materials like clear plastic, glass, and water let almost all the rays of light through. They are called **transparent** objects. Some kinds of glass and plastic are not clear. They transmit light, but the light is scattered in all directions. These objects are called **translucent**. Rocks, trees, cars, and buildings stop light. They either reflect light or absorb light. They are **opaque**. When light hits an opaque object, it casts a shadow. The dark shadow with all light blocked is called the **umbra**. The lighter shadow, when some light creeps around the edges, is called the **penumbra**. You can see the umbra and penumbra on the moon some nights and during eclipses of the Sun or moon.

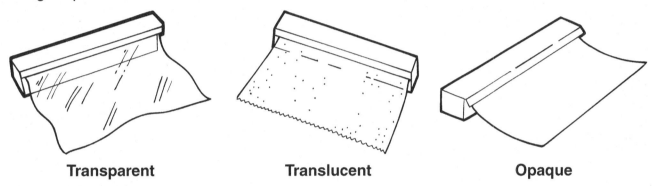

Transparent   **Translucent**   **Opaque**

SHADOWS

The size of the shadow you cast during the day depends on the angle of the sunlight, which will vary depending on the time of day. When the Sun is directly overhead near the middle of the day, it does not cast a shadow. When the Sun is lower in the sky, the shadows it casts are longer than the objects creating them. When the Sun is higher in the sky, the shadows are shorter than the objects creating them.

Facts to Remember

- *Light is composed of photons.*

- *Photons sometimes act like waves and sometimes like particles.*

- *Light is one form of electromagnetic radiation.*

- *Opaque objects cast shadows.*

- *The size of a shadow depends on the time of day.*

VOCABULARY

opaque—*does not allow light through*

penumbra—*the lighter shadow around the edges of some objects*

photons—*packages of light energy*

translucent—*light will enter but does not travel through*

transparent—*light will pass through*

umbra—*the darker part of a shadow*

Making Shadows

Materials
meterstick, yardstick, or ruler

Directions

Plan to do this activity at three times during the day—early morning, near noon, and later afternoon. You need a partner for this activity.

1. Use a meterstick, yardstick, or ruler to measure the shadow of each of the features named.

2. Measure them at the times indicated on the page.

3. Measure the actual height of any feature that you can.

4. Make the measurements in inches or centimeters.

	Morning	Noon	Afternoon	Actual Height
Tree	_____	_____	_____	_____
Pole	_____	_____	_____	_____
You	_____	_____	_____	_____
Your Partner	_____	_____	_____	_____
Ruler	_____	_____	_____	_____
Stick	_____	_____	_____	_____
Slide	_____	_____	_____	_____
Table	_____	_____	_____	_____
Baseball	_____	_____	_____	_____
Other	_____	_____	_____	_____

When are the shadows shortest? _____

When are the shadows longest? _____

Is there any shadow at noon? _____

Shadow Clock

Materials
- *play dough or modeling clay*
- *straws*
- *masking tape*
- *paper cups*
- *scissors*
- *compass*
- *5-inch square pieces of thick paper (tagboard, manila folder, etc.)*

Making the Shadow Clock

1. Cut a sheet of tagboard, manila folder, or other thick paper into a 5-inch square.

2. Use scissors or a pencil to make a small hole in the center of the bottom of the paper cup.

3. Stick one ounce of play dough or modeling clay to the center of the 5-inch square.

4. Stick the straw into the play dough or modeling clay standing as straight as possible.

5. Put a hole in the botom of the paper cup.

6. Push the top of the straw through the hole in the paper cup and bring the cup down to the 5-inch square.

7. Adjust the cup and straw until the straw is perfectly straight.

8. Tape the cup securely to the paper.

Marking the Shadow Clock

1. Mark the four sides of the shadow clock model with the directions shown in the illustration—N (north), S (south), E (east), and W (west).

2. On an outside table or sidewalk in the full sun, face the N side of the model toward the north. Use a compass to help you.

3. Notice the shadow created by the straw.

4. Exactly at the next full hour, mark the time on the card where the shadow falls.

5. Do the same every hour throughout the day.

6. Use the shadow clock for several days to determine time.

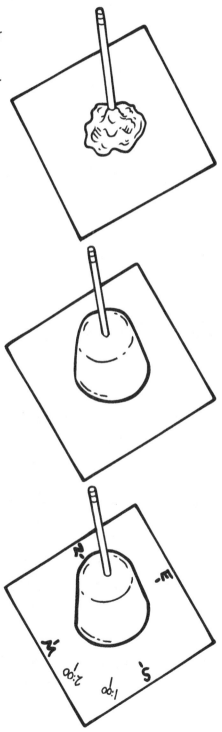

Student Inquiry Activity

This page will help you get your inquiry activity started. This activity can be done alone or by a team of two students. Students may need to do part of this activity outdoors.

Playing with Shadows

1. Make or find as many different shadows as you can.
2. Try to make darker shadows and lighter shadows.
3. Observe how long the shadows are compared to the object making the shadow.
4. Look for the position of the sun.
5. Sketch some of the shadows you made in the space below.

Inquiry Investigations with Shadows

- Do shadows get longer at different times of the day?
- How can you measure the length of tall objects making shadows?
- Is there ever a time of the day when no shadow is produced?
- When are the longest shadows produced?
- When is the shadow the exact same length as the height of the object making the shadow?
- Can you have shadows with moonlight?
- How are indoor shadows changed by the location of a flashlight in a dark place?

Write two questions you have about shadows.

1. _____

2. _____

Choosing an Investigation

Use the Student Inquiry Worksheets to help you select and plan an investigation. Your data may be in the form of sketches, measurements, and times.

Reflection of Light

DID YOU KNOW THAT . . . ?

● *Light travels at a speed of 186,000 miles per second.*

● *It takes about eight seconds for light to travel the 93 million miles from the Sun to Earth.*

● *Nothing in the universe travels faster than light.*

CHARACTERISTICS OF LIGHT

Light is a form of energy. It travels freely through the vacuum of space. The direct source of light in our solar system is the Sun. Light from the Sun and most other sources is produced by incandescence, which means it was created by hot objects. Light normally travels in a straight line until it meets objects that absorb it, bend it, or slow it down.

REFLECTION

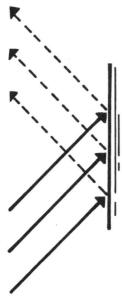

When light from the Sun or any other source meets an object, some of it bounces off. This is called *reflection*. It is this reflected light we see when we are looking at something. Of course, we do see some objects that produce light themselves, such as a fire, a lamp, or the Sun. However, we see most of the objects because they reflect light that bounces off these objects.

We often don't see gases very well because gas molecules move rapidly and don't reflect light very well. We do see liquids and solids quite well. What we see depends on two conditions: the amount of light being reflected and the texture of the object. For example, a smooth, flat, white wall reflects far more light than a dark, rough, stonewall. If a surface reflects absolutely no light, it appears black.

GOOD REFLECTORS

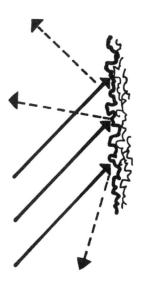

Flat, shiny surfaces reflect light well. These include such materials as mirrors, glass, and other clear, smooth objects, such as aluminum foil. Still, clear water reflects light very well. Surfaces which are flat, such as automobile bodies, windows, and mirrors, reflect light at a specific angle. Surfaces which are rough, such as crumpled aluminum foil, rocks, or rugs, reflect light at many different angles because the surface particles are facing many different directions. This is called *diffuse reflection* because the rays are diffused or spread at many different angles.

Unit 14

Reflection of Light

REFLECTION WITH MIRRORS

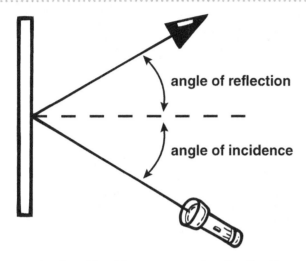

angle of reflection

angle of incidence

angle of incidence = angle of reflection

The angle at which a ray of light meets a plane (flat) mirror or any smooth surface is called the **angle of incidence**. The angle at which light strikes a mirror is exactly equal to the angle at which it is reflected off the surface. If light strikes a mirror at a 30° angle, it will reflect back at a 30° angle. If the light strikes the mirror at right angles (90°) to a mirror, it will reflect directly back at exactly 90°. Scientists say that the angle of incidence equals the **angle of reflection**.

Materials which are not smooth or polished do not illustrate this principle. The surface particles on rough surfaces are all facing in different directions and therefore reflect light in many different directions. The smooth surfaces of shiny metal, glass, or mirrors all face in the same direction, and light is reflected in one direction at the same angle. Smooth surfaces are thus the best reflectors.

MIRROR IMAGES

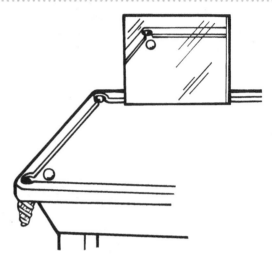

When we look at a flat mirror, the image we see seems to be as far away as we are from the mirror. When light falls on a completely smooth surface, like a mirror, all of the rays are reflected at the same angle. The image that is formed looks like it is actually behind the mirror.

Facts to Remember

- *The angle at which light hits a mirror is exactly equal to the angle of reflection.*

- *Light is a form of energy.*

- *Smooth, flat, light surfaces reflect light well.*

- *Rough, dark, textured surfaces do not reflect light well.*

VOCABULARY

angle of incidence—*the angle of light rays striking an object*

angle of reflection—*the angle of light rays bouncing off an object*

Reflection

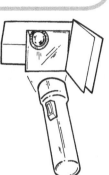

Materials
- *mirror*   • *flashlight*   • *white index card*

Directions

You need one or two partners for this activity.

1. Hold the mirror and white index card upright at right angles to each other as shown in the illustration.
2. Shine the flashlight directly at the mirror.
3. Darken the room.
4. Describe what happened to the light. Could you see the light reflected onto the card?

_____

_____

5. Move the flashlight at different angles and different distances from the mirror. Describe and illustrate below what happened to the reflection.

Illustrations

Descriptions

_____

_____

_____

Try This

Arrange the card and mirror at many different angles. Describe the reflection and illustrate the angle like shown on the right.

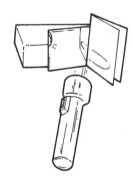

Illustrations

Descriptions

_____

_____

More Reflection

Materials
- *aluminum foil*
- *flashlight*
- *white index card*
- *sunlight*
- *mirror*
- *black construction paper*

Directions

You need one or two partners for this activity.

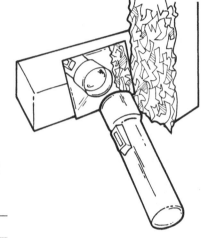

1. Hold the mirror and the shiny side of a piece of aluminum foil upright at right angles to each other as shown in the illustration.

2. Shine the flashlight directly at the mirror.

3. Darken the room.

4. Describe what happened to the light. Could you see the light reflected onto the foil?

   _____

   _____

5. Move the flashlight at different angles and different distances from the mirror. What happened to the reflection? Is the reflection brighter than on the white card you used on the previous activity?

   _____

6. Arrange the mirror and foil at different angles. Describe what happened.

   _____

   _____

7. Substitute a piece of black construction paper for the foil. Try many different angles. What is different about the black paper?

   _____

Try This

Take the mirror and all of the materials to a sunny area outside. Focus the mirror so that sunlight hits the mirror directly. Arrange the card at a right angle to the mirror. Does the sunlight reflect as well as the flashlight? _____

Try different angles with the mirror, the card, the foil, and the black paper. Describe and illustrate your results below or on the back.

_____

_____

Student Inquiry Activity

This page will help you get your inquiry activity started. This activity should be done by teams of two students.

Playing with Light

Play with a flashlight and two mirrors or other reflective material. Take turns with your partner holding the mirrors or reflectors at different angles and distances from the light.

Thinking About Reflection

- What happens when you reflect light from one mirror to another?
- How does the angle of the first mirror affect the image on the second mirror?
- What materials are very good reflectors?
- What happens when reflectors have bumps on them?
- How does changing the angle of the flashlight affect the reflection?
- How does sunlight reflect with two mirrors?
- Can you get light to reflect off water?
- Can you get light to reflect off wet surfaces?

Write two inquiry questions of your own.

Inquiry Question #1: _____

_____

Inquiry Question #2: _____

_____

Your Inquiry Investigation

Which inquiry question seems most interesting to you? Why?

_____

Which inquiry question would be the hardest to do? Why?

_____

Which inquiry investigation can you do?

_____

Describe what you will do.

_____

_____

_____

Doing the Investigation

Use the Student Inquiry Worksheets as a guideline for completing your investigation.

Refraction

DID YOU KNOW THAT . . . ?

- *An electron microscope can magnify objects to more than one million times their actual size.*

- *Light travels through air at 186,000 miles per second.*

- *Light travels through water at 140,000 miles per second.*

- *Light travels through glass at 115,000 miles per second.*

- *Light travels through a diamond at only 78,000 miles per second.*

BENDING LIGHT

Light travels in straight lines. However, light rays bend when they travel from one transparent material to another. Transparent materials like air, glass, and water are easy to see through. Rays of light bend because they travel more slowly through some substances than they do through others. For example, light travels faster through air than it does through such substances as glass or water. Therefore, when light travels from air to water, it changes directions slightly. This bending of light is called **refraction**.

OBSERVING REFRACTION

How far light bends depends on two factors: which substances it is passing through and the direction of the light as it hits the surface of the substance it is entering. Because light travels at different speeds through different materials, light bends at different angles. The direction of the light rays can also result in a different angle of refraction.

We are able to see an object because of the light that reflects from that object. When a part of an object is underwater, like the spoon in the illustration, the light from underwater changes direction as it travels from the water back into the air. The light traveling through the air above the water is coming from a different direction than the rays of light coming from the water. As a result, the spoon appears to be broken cleanly at the waterline of the glass.

Refraction

SPECIAL EFFECTS

Sometimes light enters material at such a shallow angle that it does not leave the material. It is refracted so much that the light is simply reflected inside. Light can be refracted in the air in certain conditions. Rays of light move in straight lines in cool air. However, warm air can refract light. If you are standing in a desert so that you look at light traveling through an upper layer of cool air and a lower layer of warm air, you may see **reflections** that appear to be water. This is a **mirage**, based on the ability of warm air to refract light.

USING REFRACTION

The refraction of light by some materials makes the magnification of objects in a **microscope** possible. Water is a natural magnifier because the rays of light hitting water bend apart. When the light rays are refracted, the image will appear larger. Water can **magnify** an object two to three times its real size.

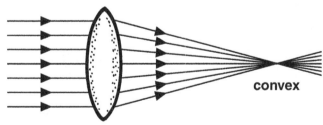
convex

A **convex** lens, like the drop of water, is a piece of glass, which is thicker in the middle than at the sides. The light coming from the mirror on a microscope travels through the glass. It is slowed down and refracted with the rays converging to make the object appear larger. The more curved a lens, the larger the object will appear to the viewer.

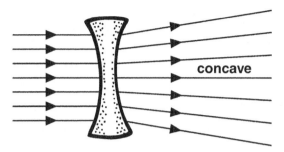
concave

A **concave** lens, which is thinner in the middle than on the sides, has the opposite effect. The light is bent and rays of light move apart making the image appear smaller.

Facts to Remember

● *Light is refracted (bent) when it travels through different materials.*

● *Light travels faster through air than through water or glass.*

● *An object can be magnified because light is refracted by glass.*

VOCABULARY

concave—*a lens which is thinner in the middle than on the edges*

convex—*a lens which bulges in the middle*

magnify—*to enlarge the appearance of an object*

microscope—*a tool to magnify the appearance of objects*

mirage—*an optical illusion*

reflection—*the bouncing of light rays off an object*

refraction—*the bending of light rays*

Refraction Using Straws

Materials
- *straws or stirrers*
- *clear, plastic cups*
- *plastic spoons, forks, or knives*
- *water*

Directions

1. Pour water into a clear, plastic cup until it is half full.
2. Place a straw or stirrer in the glass as shown in the illustration.
3. Position the straw in different directions as suggested by the illustrations below.
4. Get eye level to observe the results. Then look at the straws from different angles.
5. Complete the illustrations by drawing in the rest of the straw in each picture below.

A

B

C

D

E

F

What does it look like when the straw is straight up and down?

_____

_____

Try This

Bend the straw at an extreme angle so that it is nearly level with the surface of the water. What does it look like?

_____

Use different objects at the same angles as illustrated above. Try the following objects: pencil, different sizes of straws, ruler, plastic spoon, plastic fork, or plastic knife. Do the illustrations on the back of this paper.

Water Magnifiers

Materials
- *eyedropper*
- *ruler*
- *thin, insulated wire (from craft or hardware store)*
- *leaves, feathers, and other objects from nature*
- *plastic cups*
- *pencil*
- *water*
- *penny*
- *leaf*

Directions

1. Using an eyedropper, place a drop of water on a ruler, a pencil, and a penny. Look through the water at the lines on the ruler and the letters on the pencil and penny. Do they appear slightly larger through the drop?

2. Place a drop of water on a leaf. Do the veins under the water look slightly larger?

Making a Water Magnifier

1. Twist a short, thin piece of insulated wire over the sharpened end of a pencil to form a small circle.

2. Bend the rest of the wire into a handle for the circle. Dip the circle into a cup of water.

3. Hold it over the objects listed below. Adjust the distance of the water magnifier from the object and from your eye until you can see the enlarged image.

4. Describe what you see on each object.

   leaf: _____

   one letter in a word: _____

   feather: _____

   bark: _____

   your fingernail: _____

   a grass root: _____

   a pattern on your clothes: _____

   other objects: _____

   _____

Draw an illustration of some of the objects you magnified as they looked through the water magnifier on the back or on another sheet of paper.

Student Inquiry Activity

This page will help you get your inquiry activity started. This activity can be done alone or by a team of two students.

Getting Started

Collect some of these materials:

- clear cups and glasses of different sizes with water (half full)

• straws	• pencils	• craft sticks
• markers	• stirrers	• paper clips
• coins	• stickers	• stamps
• washers		

Inquiring Into Refraction

1. Use each of the water containers with each long object: straw, pencil, stirrer and so forth.
2. Place the objects at different angles.
3. Look for the greatest angle of refraction.
4. Look for the least angle of refraction.
5. Record your results by sketching each arrangement in the space below.

6. Examine the stamps, washers, coins, and stickers under or in water.
7. Look for the refraction and magnification.

Doing Your Inquiry Investigation

Choose your inquiry investigation about refraction and do the investigation by following the guidelines on your Student Inquiry Worksheets.

Elements

DID YOU KNOW THAT . . . ?

- *A single speck of dust floating in the air contains about 1,000,000,000,000,000 (one quadrillion) atoms.*

- *Electrons move so fast that they orbit the nucleus of an atom billions of times in a fraction of a second.*

- *There are 18,000,000,000,000 (18 trillion) tons of sodium in the oceans.*

- *Nitrogen is the most abundant element in Earth's atmosphere. About 78% of the atmosphere is nitrogen.*

- *The most common element in the universe is hydrogen. Helium is the next most common.*

- *It would take 17,000,000,000,000,000,000,000,000 (17 septillion) atoms of hydrogen to weigh an ounce (the weight of five sheets of paper).*

ATOMS

An **atom** is an extremely tiny particle of matter. Everything that exists is made up of atoms. Atoms are so small that a million of

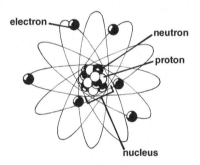

them would fit in the period at the end of this sentence. Within atoms are three types of even smaller particles. Each atom contains a **nucleus**, or center, which contains **protons** and **neutrons**. **Electrons** orbit around this nucleus. Two of these particles have electrical charges. A proton has a positive electrical charge. An electron has a negative charge. A neutron has no charge at all. Usually, each atom has the same number of protons and electrons so that it is neither positively nor negatively charged.

ELEMENTS

There are 92 naturally occurring atoms called **elements**. Each element has a different arrangement of atoms. Each element has only one kind of atom. An atom of gold always has the same number (79) of protons. An atom of carbon always has 6 protons. The atom usually has the same number of electrons as it does protons. There are 92 natural elements in the universe and 24 elements that have been created by scientists in laboratories.

PERIODIC TABLE

The chemical elements are arranged on a periodic table that gives their names, chemical symbols, and atomic numbers. Elements are arranged in order by their atomic number in 18 columns (groups) and 9 rows. Elements that behave in a similar way are close to each other in groups on the table. Elements are placed in rows according to the arrangement of electrons around the nucleus of the atom.

Unit 16

Elements

THE PERIODIC TABLE

This version of the periodic table gives the atomic number, the symbol, and the name of the elements.

Periodic Table

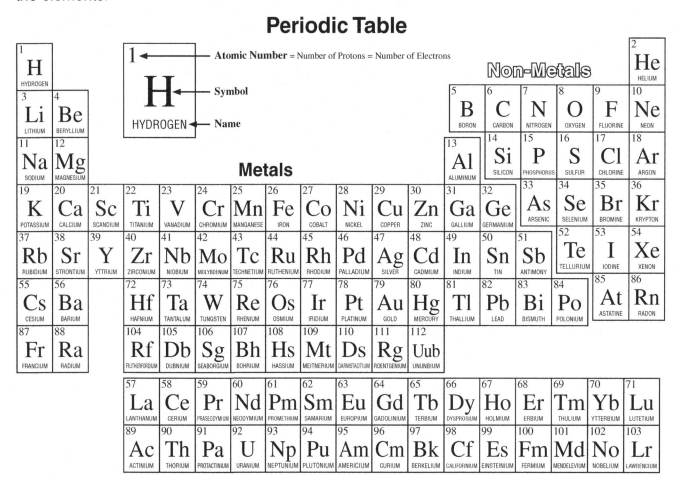

Facts to Remember

- Everything in the universe is made up of atoms.

- Atoms have protons, neutrons, and electrons.

- The periodic table lists the natural elements in the universe.

VOCABULARY

atom—*tiny particle of matter*

electron—*negatively charged particle orbiting the nucleus of an atom*

element—*a material composed of only one type of atom*

neutron—*particle with no charge in an atom*

nucleus—*the center of an atom with protons and neutrons*

proton—*positively-charged particle in the nucleus of an atom*

Practice with the Periodic Table

Directions: Use the Periodic Table on page 96 to fill in the information about these common elements.

Nitrogen
Colorless, odorless gas
Most common element in Earth's atmosphere
Essential element in plant growth
Atomic Number: _____   Symbol: _____

Oxygen
Colorless, odorless gas
About 20% of Earth's atmosphere
Essential for survival of most living things
Atomic Number: _____   Symbol: _____

Carbon
Non-metallic element
Exists in tissue of all living things
Most forms of carbon are black like charcoal
Atomic Number: _____   Symbol: _____

Iron
Silvery white metal (when pure iron)
Used in making many products
Easily combines with other elements
Atomic Number: _____   Symbol: _____

Calcium
Silvery metallic element
Essential for bones and teeth
Important element in seashells, chalk, lime, and cement
Atomic Number: _____   Symbol: _____

Gold
Soft, heavy metal
Used in jewelry, coins, and teeth
Atomic Number: _____   Symbol: _____

Hydrogen
Colorless, odorless gas
Most common element in the universe
Basic source of the Sun's heat
Atomic Number: _____   Symbol: _____

Sodium
Silver metallic element
Element in salt and baking soda
Atomic Number: _____   Symbol: _____

More Practice with the Periodic Table

Directions: Find the names on the Periodic Table to match the symbols listed below. Use the Periodic Table on page 96 to help answer the questions.

Au _____   O _____   He _____

H _____   Ra _____   Zn _____

Na _____   U _____   Sn _____

Fe _____   Pb _____   K _____

I _____   Kr _____   N _____

Ag _____   Cu _____   Al _____

Ni _____   Ne _____   Cl _____

Directions: Find the atomic number for these elements on the Periodic Table.

Calcium _____   Oxygen _____   Helium _____

Iron _____   Aluminum _____   Copper _____

Phosphorus _____   Sodium _____   Silicon _____

Gold _____   Mercury _____   Carbon _____

Uranium _____   Aluminum _____   Nitrogen _____

Boron _____   Lead _____   Iodine _____

Directions: Find the name to match these atomic numbers on the Periodic Table.

1 _____   13 _____   16 _____

92 _____   12 _____   17 _____

30 _____   28 _____   50 _____

53 _____   22 _____   74 _____

10 _____   36 _____   8 _____

Compounds

DID YOU KNOW THAT . . . ?

- *A liter of any gas, such as oxygen, at normal temperature and pressure may contain 26,000,000,000,000,000,000,000 (26 sextillion) molecules.*

- *Pure 24 carat gold is an element.*

- *Bread is a mixture of a solid and a gas.*

- *Salt is a compound of a poisonous gas (chlorine) and a metal (sodium).*

MOLECULES

A **molecule** is the smallest particle of an element or a compound that can exist on its own. A molecule is formed when two or more elements are held together by a chemical action called **bonding**. The electrons in the **atoms** create the molecular bond by their actions.

MIXTURES

Mixtures are two or more materials that are not chemically bound together. Bread, shaving cream, soapy water, hair gel, and some salad dressings are examples of mixtures. The individual substances can usually be separated easily. In a mixture, the atoms of different elements do not combine chemically.

COMPOUNDS

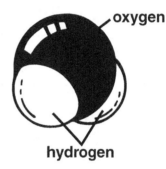

oxygen

hydrogen

A **compound** is a chemical combination of two or more elements held together in molecules that are exactly alike. The chemical bonds that hold molecules of a compound together are not easily broken. Chemists use formulas to identify the make up of each molecule. The formula specifies how many atoms of each element are combined to make the compound. Water is the chemical bonding of two atoms of hydrogen and one atom of oxygen in each molecule of water. The formula for water is H_2O. There are millions of other compounds, some produced by nature and others in scientific laboratories.

Unit
17

Compounds

COMMON COMPOUNDS

Sodium Chloride (NaCl)

This is the chemical name for table salt. Salt is an essential compound for many creatures, including humans. It was so valuable in Roman times that soldiers were often paid in salt.

NaCl—The chemical name indicates that for every atom of sodium, there is one atom of chlorine.

Calcium Carbonate (CaCO$_3$)

This is the chemical name for chalk used for blackboards. It is formed in seashells and bones

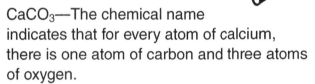

CaCO$_3$—The chemical name indicates that for every atom of calcium, there is one atom of carbon and three atoms of oxygen.

Hydrogen Peroxide (H$_2$O$_2$)

This is a liquid used for bleaching and disinfecting.

H$_2$O$_2$—The chemical name for this compound indicates that for every two atoms of hydrogen, there are two atoms of oxygen.

Acetic Acid (C$_2$H$_4$O$_2$)

This is the chemical name for vinegar that is used for cooking and other household uses.

C$_2$H$_4$O$_2$—The name indicates that two atoms of carbon, four atoms of hydrogen, and two atoms of oxygen form every molecule of vinegar.

Sulfuric Acid (H$_2$SO$_4$)

Sulfuric acid is one of the most important industrial chemicals. It is used in automobile batteries, explosives, oil refining, making paper, and many other products.

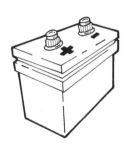

H$_2$SO$_4$—The chemical name indicates that for every two atoms of hydrogen, there is one atom of sulfur, and four atoms of oxygen.

Facts to Know

● *Mixtures and compounds are chemically different.*

● *Elements are arranged on the Periodic Table.*

● *There are millions of different compounds.*

● *All of the molecules in a specific compound are alike.*

VOCABULARY

atom—*a tiny particle of matter*

bonding—*the chemical union of two or more elements*

compound—*a substance consisting of two or more elements held together by chemical bonds*

mixture—*two or more substances which are not chemically united*

molecule—*the smallest particle of an element or compound which can exist on its own*

Understanding Compounds

Directions: Some common compounds are listed below. Use the formulas given, the samples on page 100, and the Periodic Table on page 96 to list the elements in each compound. The first one has been done for you.

Water (H_2O)
Water is essential to all living things on Earth.
Each molecule contains: two atoms of hydrogen and one atom of oxygen.

Ammonia (NH_3)
This is a strong cleaning agent that is also used in fertilizers, explosives, and refrigeration.
Each molecule contains: _____

_____

Iron Oxide (Fe_2O_3)
This is the chemical name for rust.
Each molecule contains: _____

_____

Sugar ($C_6H_{12}O_6$)
This is a chemical essential to plants and animals.
Each molecule contains: _____

_____

Boric Acid (H_3BO_3)
This acid is used to kill germs and bugs and is in eye drops.
Each molecule contains: _____

_____

Silicon Dioxide (SiO_2)
This is the chemical name for quartz used in watches.
Each molecule contains: _____

_____

Carbon Dioxide (CO_2)
Plants use carbon dioxide, and animals exhale it.
Each molecule contains: _____

_____

Carbon Monoxide (CO)
This is a deadly gas in automobile exhaust.
Each molecule contains: _____

_____

Bismuth Oxychloride (BiOCl)
This is used to make lipstick, eye shadow, and nail polish look frosted.
Each molecule contains: _____

_____

Benjamin Franklin

Benjamin Franklin was the most famous American in the world during the late 1700s. He was as well known and admired for his scientific interests as for his efforts in creating a new nation, the United States of America. A highly respected scientist, Franklin studied electricity, weather, ocean currents, such as the Gulf Stream, and many other scientific subjects. Franklin was one of the wealthiest men in Pennsylvania when he retired in his early 40s from the printing business and devoted his life to public service. He started the first fire department and first public library in America and helped create what became the University of Pennsylvania.

Franklin's famous kite experiment proved that lightning is a form of static electricity. He used his understanding of electricity to invent the lightning rod, which protected homes and barns from being struck by lightning and burned. Franklin invented such terms as *battery, electric shock, positive charge*, and *negative charge* to describe the behavior of electricity. He once used a Leyden jar that could store static electricity to electrocute a turkey and to give an electrical shock to his friends.

Franklin studied heat and the movement of air currents. He used the results of his studies to invent an iron furnace called the *Franklin Stove*, which was much more efficient and safer than the fireplaces used in colonial America. It used less wood and was less likely to catch a house on fire.

Ben Franklin had trouble reading as he got older. He cut the lenses of glasses so that the lower part of each lens could be used for reading and the upper part for seeing at greater distances. These bifocal glasses were a major contribution to modern medicine. Franklin enjoyed music so much that he invented a musical instrument called the *glass armonica*, which could be played somewhat like a piano. The famous composer, Wolfgang Amadeus Mozart, actually wrote music to be played on this instrument.

Franklin was very interested in weather patterns. In the mid 1740s, he noted that northeast storms started in the southwest, exactly opposite to what seemed likely. He once chased a storm on horseback in order to learn more about them. Franklin wanted to use daylight more efficiently and invented the concept of Daylight Savings Time, which is still widely used.

Franklin was a witness to the first manned balloon flight in November of 1783 in Paris. The Montgolfier brothers had invented a hot air balloon that carried two French noblemen into the air. He predicted accurately that these balloons would be used in the future for military spying, dropping bombs, and studying weather. Franklin was truly a scientist for the ages.

Static Electricity

DID YOU KNOW THAT . . . ?

- *Lightning is a gigantic spark of static electricity in the atmosphere.*

- *The word electricity comes from the Greek word for amber, a fossil made from hardened tree sap. When amber was rubbed with cloth, small objects stuck to it.*

WHAT IS STATIC ELECTRICITY?

Static electricity was the first kind of electricity to be discovered and the only kind known until the last two hundred years. Static electricity is an electric charge that does not flow in an electric current from a battery or along an electric wire to light a bulb or some other electric tool. Static electricity is a charge that stays in one place.

FRICTION MAKES THE CHARGE

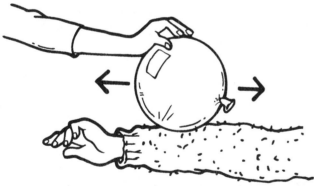

Static electricity can be produced by **friction** when two materials are rubbed together. During the process of rubbing, **electrons** can be rubbed off from the atoms of one material and onto the atoms of another material. The materials used to create a static charge must be electrical insulators, materials that do not conduct electricity. If they were conductors, like copper, aluminum, or water, the charge would just flow away. Some common insulators that create static charges are rubber, cloth, hair, and plastic.

ELECTRONS MAKE THE DIFFERENCE

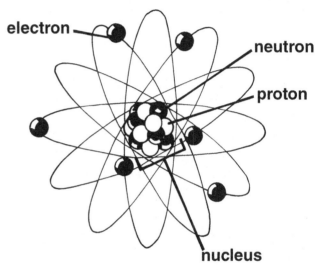

Materials are made of atoms united in chemical compounds. The atoms in these materials are neutral because they have the same number of **positively-charged** protons as they do of **negatively-charged** electrons. However, if atoms gain electrons, they become negatively charged because they now have more negatively-charged electrons than positively-charged protons. If atoms lose electrons, they then become positively-charged because they have more positively-charged protons than negatively-charged electrons. If an object has either a positive or a negative charge, it can produce static electricity.

Unit 18

Static Electricity

RECOGNIZING STATIC ELECTRICITY

Static electricity often produces a crackling sound and sometimes a spark. You may hear it when you fold the laundry or take off a sweater. Rubbing your shoes across the carpet and then touching a light switch may produce a static charge and a spark. These activities always involve rubbing or friction of some type.

EXPERIMENTING WITH STATIC ELECTRICITY

You cannot always tell when objects have a positive or negative charge because it is difficult to know if electrons have been rubbed off from an object or onto an object. When a balloon is rubbed against cloth, it collects electrons and therefore has a negative charge.

CHARGES ATTRACT AND REPEL

If you have two objects with a negative charge, they will **repel** (push away) each other just like two negative poles of a magnet will repel each other. If you have two objects with a positive charge, they will also repel each other. However, if one object is positively charged, and the other is negatively charged, they will **attract** each other just like opposite poles of a magnet attract each other.

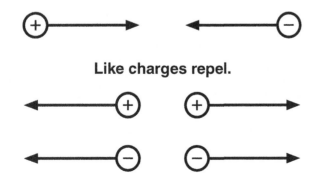

Opposite charges attract.

Like charges repel.

If one object has either a positive or a

negative charge like the balloons in the experiments on the next two pages, it will attract objects that are neutral (have no charge at all). The pepper, flakes, glitter, and salt have no charge in the experiments on pages 105 and 106. They are attracted to the balloon that does have a charge. Two balloons with the same charge will repel each other. Two balloons with different charges will attract each other. A charged balloon will also be attracted to a balloon with no charge.

Facts to Remember

- *Static electricity is produced by friction.*
- *Electrons can be rubbed onto or off an object.*
- *Two materials with the same charge repel each other.*
- *Two materials with different charges are attracted to each other.*
- *An object with no charge will be attracted to a charged object.*

VOCABULARY

attract—*to be pulled toward an object*

electron—*a negatively-charged particle in an atom*

friction—*rubbing of two materials against each other*

negative charge—*a charge with added electrons*

positive charge—*a charge with electrons removed*

repel—*to push away*

static electricity—*electricity staying in one place*

Creating Static Electricity

Materials
- *salt*
- *pepper*
- *glitter*
- *balloons of various sizes*
- *paper plate*
- *parsley flakes*
- *tissue*
- *spoon*

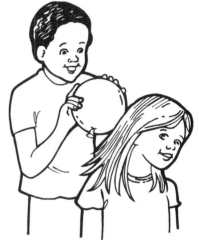

Directions

1. Blow up a balloon until it is full but not ready to pop.
2. Rub the balloon along your hair 30 times in one direction only.
3. Use a long, sweeping circular motion.
4. Be sure to rub in one direction only. Do not go back and forth. It can erase the static charge you are trying to collect.
5. Pour about a teaspoon of salt on a paper plate.
6. Pour some pepper onto the plate and stir the salt and pepper.
7. Hold the balloon above the plate.

Observations

Describe what happened to the pepper flakes. _____

_____

Did some of the salt get attracted to the balloon? How much? _____

Watch the pepper flakes on the balloon. Do any of them appear to leap off? _____

Try This

Add some glitter, parsley flakes, or other flakes to the plate. Which flakes does the balloon pick up? _____

_____

Tear up pieces of tissue. Will the balloon pick up larger pieces of tissue?

_____

Try different sides of the balloon. Does one part of the balloon appear more powerful?

_____

Describe what happened.

_____

_____

Comparing Static Electricity

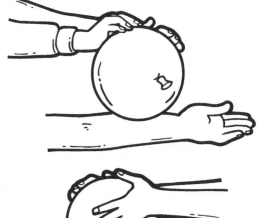

Materials
- *balloons of various sizes*
- *paper plate*
- *salt*
- *pepper*

Directions

1. Blow up a balloon until it is full but not ready to pop.
2. Rub the balloon along your bare arm 30 times in one direction only.
3. Use a long, sweeping circular motion.
4. Be sure to rub in one direction only. Do not go back and forth. It can erase the static charge you are trying to collect.
5. Make a plate of pepper and salt as you did in the previous activity.

Which rubbing charged the balloon better with more static electricity—your hair or your arm? How can you tell? _____

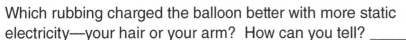

_____

Try These

Rub the balloon 30 times along your pants or your leg. Test the balloon over the salt-and-pepper plate. Describe your results. _____

_____

Rub the balloon 30 times along your sweater or your shirt. Test the balloon over the salt-and-pepper plate. Describe your results. _____

_____

Rub the balloon 30 times along a friend's hair. Test the balloon over the salt-and-pepper plate. Describe your results. _____

_____

Drawing Conclusions

What conclusions can you draw from your experiments? _____

_____

_____

Which styles of hair seem better at producing static electricity? Why? _____

_____

Student Inquiry Activity

This page will help you get your inquiry activity started. This activity can be done alone or by a team of two students. Use the Student Inquiry Worksheets for a guideline as you complete this inquiry activity.

Static Electricity on the Brain

What is the biggest static charge you can generate using some of the materials below or others you can get?

large balloons	long, thin balloons	water balloons
hair	socks	wool scarf
bare arm	nylon jacket	stockings
jeans	t-shirt	tennis shoes
salt	pepper	cereal flakes

How did you do the investigation? _____

_____

_____

_____

How did you test your results? _____

_____

_____

_____

More Ideas

- What is the longest-lasting static charge you can make?
- What materials can you use to make a static charge?
- What materials are very poor for making a static charge?
- How could you make two static charges that attract each other?
- How could you make two static charges that repel (push away) each other?

Doing Your Inquiry Investigation

Use one of the inquiry questions suggested above or a question of your own to test in an inquiry investigation. Use the Student Inquiry Worksheets to help you do your investigation.

Unit 19

Lightning

HOW LIGHTNING HAPPENS

Lightning is a powerful spark of natural electricity caused by the build up of electric charges in thick, heavy clouds. Thunderclouds are formed when warm, wet air rises rapidly and then quickly cools high in the sky. Inside the cloud, water drops and ice particles bump each other and build up static electricity by knocking electrons off some particles.

Small particles with a positive charge move to the top of a cloud. Larger particles with a negative charge sink to the bottom of a cloud. This negative charge in the lower portion of a cloud can attract a positive charge from the ground. When a positive charge and a negative charge interact, lightning is the result. When the difference between the charges is great, a bolt of lightning will occur either between the top and bottom of the cloud with their opposite charges, between two clouds, or between the bottom of the cloud and the ground.

The electrical discharge often takes a forked shape because it is following the line of least resistance through the clouds. This is called **fork lightning**. If it is hidden behind or within a cloud, the forked pattern is diffused and glows. This is called **sheet lightning**.

When lightning hits the earth, it often hits the tallest feature in the area, such as a tree, hill, or building. Buildings, especially very tall ones, are often protected by lightning rods, which were first invented by Benjamin Franklin. A rod is placed on top of a building with a wire leading down to a rod in the ground. Lightning's fierce jolt of electricity is carried harmlessly away from the structure into the ground.

Thunder is heard because the lightning heats the air so hot that the air rapidly expands at a speed faster than the speed of sound. This creates the sound of thunder.

Lightning

SAFETY IN A LIGHTNING STORM

Lightning kills and injures more people in the United States most years than any other type of weather except floods. There is no completely safe place to be in a lightning storm, but some places are especially dangerous. Follow these safety procedures in an electrical storm.

1. Do not stand under or near a tree or any other tall object. Do not stand near or under flagpoles, tents, communications towers, and light poles. Lightning is attracted to the tallest objects in an open field.

2. Do not go in or near bodies of water, such as oceans, lakes, rivers, and streams. Lightning is an electrical charge and is attracted to water.

3. Do not sit in golf carts, convertible cars, tractors, truck beds, or other open spaces in vehicles.

4. Do not lie flat in an open field. Kneel and bend down keeping your head lower than your back.

5. Seek safety in large, closed buildings. These are much safer than smaller open shelters.

6. You can find protection in fully enclosed motor vehicles such as cars and trucks. Don't touch the outer metal surfaces during storms.

7. When you are inside a house during an electrical storm, do not touch metal window frames, plumbing fixtures and pipes, electrical outlets and cords, telephones, televisions, cable TV wires, and similar electric fixtures.

Facts to Know

- *Lightning is a natural form of static electricity.*

- *Lightning often hits the tallest object in an area.*

- *Lightning is formed by the interaction of positive and negative charges within clouds.*

- *Thunder is created when heated air expands faster than the speed of sound.*

VOCABULARY

fork lightning—*streaks of lightning that follow the line of least resistance through the cloud*

sheet lightning—*lightning that glows and is hidden or diffused in a cloud*

Balloon Attraction

Materials
- *balloons of various sizes*
- *fishing line or string*

Directions

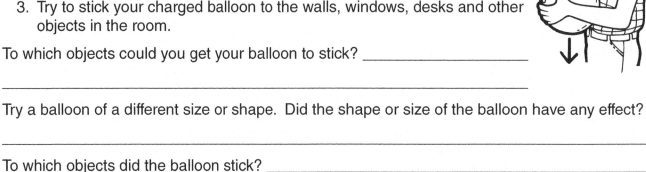

1. Blow up a balloon until it is full but not ready to pop.
2. Rub the balloon along your hair, sweater, arm, or clothes 30 times in one direction only. Use a long, sweeping circular motion. Be sure to rub in one direction only. Do not go back and forth. It can erase the static charge you are trying to collect.
3. Try to stick your charged balloon to the walls, windows, desks and other objects in the room.

To which objects could you get your balloon to stick? _____

_____

Try a balloon of a different size or shape. Did the shape or size of the balloon have any effect?

_____

To which objects did the balloon stick? _____

_____

Directions

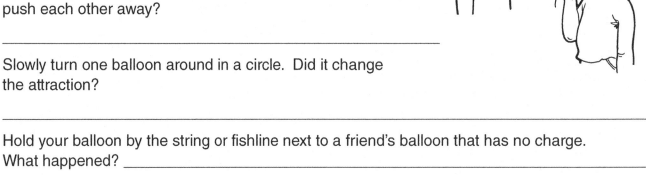

1. Tie a 1-foot long string or piece of fishline to the tie of the balloon. Have a partner do the same.
2. Rub your balloon 30 times one way against your favorite material for getting a static charge. Have your partner do the same.
3. Hold your balloon by the string or fishline next to your partner's balloon that has also been rubbed with a charge.

What happened to the balloons. Did they attract each other or push each other away?

_____

Slowly turn one balloon around in a circle. Did it change the attraction?

_____

Hold your balloon by the string or fishline next to a friend's balloon that has no charge. What happened? _____

_____

Making an Electroscope

An electroscope can be used to detect the presence of a static charge.

> **Materials**
> - *clear, plastic cup*
> - *manila folder*
> - *sandpaper*
> - *masking tape*
> - *scissors*
> - *balloon*
> - *aluminum foil*
> - *pushpin*
> - *3-inch piece of bare copper wire*

Directions

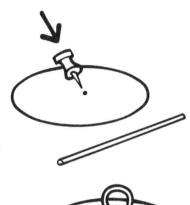

1. Cut a piece of manila folder to make a round cover for the clear, plastic cup.

2. Use the sandpaper or scissors to scrape the plastic coating from a 3-inch piece of copper wire if it is not already bare.

3. Use the pushpin to make a small hole in the center of the lid you cut out.

4. Make a loop with the wire and push the pointed end of the wire through the hole in the lid so that it extends down about one inch. Use a piece of masking tape around the wire at the hole so that it does not slip.

5. Fold the two prongs of wire up in opposite directions.

6. Cut out two square centimeter pieces of aluminum foil. Be sure the pieces are very small and light.

7. Use the pushpin to make a hole at the top of each piece of foil. Hook one piece of foil on each wire hook. Tape the lid tightly onto the plastic cup.

Using the Electroscope

- Inflate a balloon, tie it, and rub it along your hair, sweater, or another article of clothing about 30 times to create a static charge. Touch the loop of wire above the cup with the balloon.

- Observe the pieces of foil. They should push apart because they are both receiving the same charge. Like charges repel each other just as the same poles of a magnet repel each other.

- You can also hold the balloon next to the plastic side of the cup and notice how the foil pieces are attracted toward the balloon.

Unit 20

Properties of Water

DID YOU KNOW THAT . . . ?

● *On a summer day, a giant oak can drink 300 gallons of water.*

● *Water can climb three feet up a tree in one minute on a hot summer day.*

● *Water is very heavy. A cubic foot of water—the amount in a container one foot long, one foot wide, and one foot high—weighs over 62 pounds.*

CAPILLARY ACTION

Capillary action is the movement of water up very thin tubes like the tubes within the roots and stems of a flower or a tree. These tubes are called **capillaries**. The narrower the  tube within these structures, the higher the water will rise. The surface tension of water is responsible for this capillary action. There is an attraction between the molecules of water and the sides of the tubes. This action is also aided by the attraction of water molecules for each other. This attraction pulls more water into the tubes.

Water will rise in a tree or tube until the weight of the water or gravity is balanced by the surface tension. However, plants and trees also use another process called *transpiration* in which they give off water vapor through the leaves. This process acts like a **siphon** pulling more and more water up through the tubes of trees and plants.

MAKING A PIPETTE

When a scientist uses a **pipette**, this principle of capillary action is what allows the pipette to work. A pipette is a tube, like a straw or an eyedropper, that can  be used to move small amounts of water or other liquids from one container to another. Usually the pipette holds about 5 milliliters (5 cubic centimeters) at one time.

An eyedropper is pushed into a cup of water. The rubber tip is squeezed tight which removes the air and creates a vacuum. When the rubber tip is released, water flows into the bottom of the dropper and pushes air from the plastic tube into the rubber tip.

When a straw is pushed into the water, the air is pushed out and water fills the straw in the water. Keeping a finger over the top of the straw keeps the pressure equal at both ends of the straw. When the top hole is covered, the air below the bottom hole of the straw pushes up harder than the water pushes down. The straw therefore holds the water. Uncover the top hole of the straw, and the air above the hole pushes down on the air and water in the straw. The water then falls out of the straw.

Properties of Water

SIPHONS

A siphon is a tube used to move water from a higher level to a lower level. Water does not naturally flow uphill unless some pressure is used to force the water to move. Water does flow downhill because of the force of gravity.

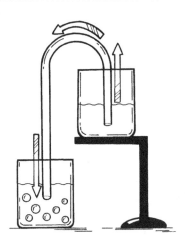

Water flows down a tube if the tube is empty of air. To make a siphon, empty a plastic tube of air. The air inside a tube can be removed by sucking when the end of the tube is inside a container of water. The air inside the tube can be removed by forcing out the air and forcing in the water as you would do when placing a tube in a container of water, where the weight of the water forces out the lighter air. You can see the bubbles of air as they leave the tube.

HOW SIPHONS WORK

Once a siphon has been emptied of air by sucking out the air or filling the tube with water, it will continue to flow because of pressure differences at the two ends of the tube. The water pressure at the higher end of the tube inserted into a container of water is greater than at the lower end. Pressure of the air on the water in the higher container pushes the water into the tube. Gravity pulls the water down the tube and into the lower container. Water will continue to flow through the tube until the water in the higher container is emptied, until the ends of the tube are at the same level, or until one end of the tube comes out of the water.

You can reverse the flow of water by reversing the heights of the cups. Keep the siphon securely in the water. Do not allow air to enter the siphon or you will have to empty out the air again. If you empty the higher cup or remove one end of the tubing, you will have to start again by filling the tube with water.

Facts to Remember

● *Capillary action carries water up the roots and stems of a plant.*

● *A siphon can carry water uphill before carrying water to a lower level.*

● *A siphon must be emptied of air before it will work.*

VOCABULARY

capillary—*a very thin tube in a plant*

pipette—*a tube used to move small amounts of a fluid*

siphon—*a tube used to carry water from a higher level to a lower level*

Making Pipettes

Materials
- *plastic or paper drinking cups*
- *1 oz. or 2 oz. cups or soufflé cups*
- *straws (different sizes)*
- *water*

Directions

1. Pour water into a plastic or paper cup of any size until it is almost full.
2. Place an empty, small 1- or 2-oz. cup next to the full cup.
3. Push a straw into the water until it touches the bottom.
4. Place your index finger firmly over the top of the straw sealing the opening.
5. Use your thumb and middle finger to lift the straw clear out of the water and hold it over the small cup.
6. Take your index finger off the top opening of the straw.

Describe what happened.

_____

_____

Try This

1. Practice with the straw pipette (little pipe) until you are skilled at lifting water with the pipette and putting it in the little cup.
2. Empty the little cup.
3. Find the one-ounce line on the cup. (It may say 30 mm.) If it is a two-ounce cup, mark a line halfway up the cup.
4. Use the straw pipette to fill the little cup to the one-ounce mark. Be slow and careful.

How many pipettes did you use? _____

How much of the straw can you fill with water? _____

Try using the straw at a different angle. Does it work better or worse?

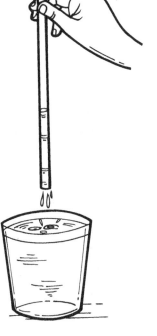

_____

What happens if you don't cover the top of the straw? _____

_____

Will it work with a smaller straw? _____

Will it work with a thinner straw? _____

What did you learn from this activity? _____

_____

Using Siphons

Materials
- *flexible tubing pieces about 1 foot long or flex straws*
- *tub or pail of water*
- *paper or plastic cups*

Directions

You need a partner for this activity.

1. Pour water into two cups until they are half full.
2. Use a piece of flexible tubing or tightly connect two flex straws. (See illustration on the right.)
3. Dip the tube or hooked straws completely into a container of water. Wait until all of the air bubbles have stopped coming out of the ends.
4. Keep one finger on each end of the tube and pull it from the water.
5. Place each end of the tube in separate cups of water and then release your fingers from the ends of the straw.

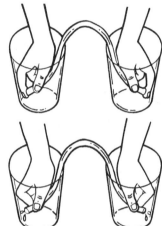

Using the Siphon

Start with the cups at an equal level. One partner should raise one cup. Does the water from the higher cup run down the tube to the lower cup? _____

_____

Raise the lower cup and lower the higher cup. Does the water reverse and flow to the lower cup? _____

If the straw empties or a cup empties, fill the siphon again and start over.

Practice with the Siphon

Use your siphon several times until you and your partner are good at raising and lowering the water level in both cups without drawing air into the siphon.

What happens if both cups are at exactly the same height?

_____

What happened if the cups were just an inch or two different in height?

_____

Try filling one cup from the tub of water using the siphon. Describe what happened.

_____

_____

Student Inquiry Activity

This page will help you get your inquiry activity started. This activity usually requires a team of two students. Use the Student Inquiry Worksheets for a guideline as you complete this inquiry activity.

Investigating Siphons

What is the fastest-flowing siphon you can make?

_____

_____

What is the longest siphon you can make that still works?

_____

_____

Can you make a working siphon with flex straws?

_____

_____

Can you make a siphon that waters a garden or a terrarium?

_____

_____

Can you make a self-starting siphon where you don't have to push out the air from the tube yourself?

_____

_____

How high can you make water flow up a siphon tube?

_____

_____

Adding Your Ideas

What can you try to do with a siphon? List some ideas.

   1. _____

   2. _____

   3. _____

Starting Your Investigation

Use the Student Inquiry Worksheets to help you choose your inquiry investigation, plan the steps, and record your results.

Surface Tension of Water

DID YOU KNOW THAT . . . ?

- *There are 1,700,000,000,000,000,000,000,000 **molecules** in a single drop of water. The number is read 1.7 **septillion**.*

- *Surface tension allows water molecules to climb up trees.*

COHESION OF WATER MOLECULES

The **molecules** in a single drop of water are strongly attracted to each other and pull together from all directions—above, below, and from every side. This tendency of water molecules is called **cohesion**. You can feel this cohesive tension of water when you cup your hand and pull it through water. One of the reasons you can float in water or swim without simply falling to the bottom and staying there is the cohesive tendency of water molecules.

SURFACE TENSION OF WATER

The cohesion of water molecules at the surface of the water is especially strong. Because water molecules at the surface of a liquid have no molecules attracting them from above, the attraction from the molecules on all sides is even greater. This creates a surface tension which has very special features. The

thin "skin" of water on the surface of water is so strong that it will hold the weight of several different kinds of insects which are adapted to walking on water. These include water striders and water skaters. The force of gravity pulling down on the insect is not as strong as the surface tension of the molecules in the water the insect is walking on.

THE MENISCUS

When you overfill a glass of water, you can see a bubble formed above the rim of the glass. It is especially easy to see if you kneel so that you are at eye level with the rim of the glass. The scientific name for this bubble is the **meniscus**. The meniscus is created by the strong attraction of water molecules for each other at the surface. This surface tension allows you to pour more water into the glass than it will hold. The meniscus is curved up like a bubble when the water is above the glass. The meniscus will curve down when the water is below the rim of the glass because the molecules of water are strongly attracted to the surface of the glass or plastic.

Unit
21

Surface Tension of Water

BREAKING SURFACE TENSION

The surface tension of water creates a strong skin on the surface of water, but that skin can be easily broken. You can break the surface tension by touching the skin with your finger. (However, if you are very careful, the surface will bend slightly before breaking.) Any sharp object such as the point of a pencil will break the surface tension. Some chemicals, such as dish soap, other detergents, and alcohol are very effective at breaking surface tension.

SOAPY WATER

The molecules in soap and alcohol combine with the water molecules and break some of the bonds that hold water molecules together. Soap, for example, makes water "wetter" meaning that it seeps into, under, and around things better. For this reason, soap and water make a better cleaner together than water does alone. When soap or alcohol drops are placed on the surface of the meniscus, the bubble breaks and anything held on the meniscus by surface tension sinks into the cup.

WATER DROPS

Evidence for surface tension is the shape of water drops. The tendency of water molecules to pull inward toward each other creates the round shape of the drop. This is the smallest and tightest possible shape. A drop that is falling down a surface usually is more stretched out. This shape occurs because the forces of gravity making the drop fall and the friction from the object it is on pull against the surface tension.

Facts to Remember

● *The meniscus is the bubble formed on the surface of a full glass of water.*

● *The meniscus may be curved down or up.*

● *Surface tension of water is the strong attraction of water molecules for each other on the surface of water.*

● *Cohesion is the attraction of water molecules for each other below the surface of water.*

● *Alcohol and soap can break the surface tension of water.*

VOCABULARY

cohesion—*a tendency to stick together*

meniscus—*a curved surface of a liquid*

molecule—*the smallest particle of a compound like water*

septillion—*a trillion times a trillion*

Surface Tension of Water

Materials
- *eyedroppers or pipettes*
- *metric ruler*
- *clear plastic cups (preferable) – 2 sizes*
- *extra cups*
- *paper towels*

Directions

1. Fill a plastic cup with water even with the rim.
2. Pour a cup about half full of water.
3. Practice filling the eyedropper or pipette about half full. (Squeeze the rubber tip of the eyedropper and insert the dropper into the partial cup of water. Release the rubber tip and the dropper should be about half full of water.)
4. Use the eyedropper or pipette to add water to the full cup. Count how many droppers or pipettes of water you can add to the full cup before it overflows.
5. Do at least three trials and record below.

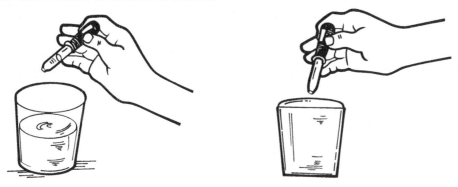

First trial: _____   Second trial: _____   Third trial: _____

Eye Level

Kneel so that you are at eye level with the glass just before it is ready to spill. You should see the bubble above the cup. It is called the *meniscus*. Hold a metric ruler next to the lip of the cup. How many millimeters high is the meniscus? _____

Try Again

Do the experiment at the top of the page again, but use a different size or style of cup. Do three trials. Record the results.

First trial: _____   Second trial: _____   Third trial: _____

More Surface Tension of Water

Materials
- *plastic and paper cups*
- *eyedroppers or pipettes*
- *alcohol*
- *dish soap*
- *paper towels*
- *paper or plastic cups*

Directions

1. Place the biggest drop of water you can make on your desk. Gently touch it with your pencil or your finger. Describe what happened.

   _____

2. Place another large drop of water on a dry part of your desk. Use an eyedropper or pipette to add a drop of dish soap to the drop. Describe what happened.

   _____

3. Fill a cup of water to the rim as you did in the experiments on page 119. Use the eyedropper or pipette to add water until the meniscus is very noticeable.

4. Add one drop of dish soap to the meniscus. Did any water spill?_____ How much? _____

5. Add another drop of dish soap to the meniscus. Describe what happened.

   _____

Try This

Fill a cup with water and make the meniscus as you have done before. Just before you think the water will spill, add a single drop of alcohol to the meniscus. Observe the results. Describe what happened.

_____

Do this experiment several more times. Alcohol and dish soap both break the surface tension of water. Based on your experiments, which do you think works quicker—alcohol or dish soap? Explain your reasons.

_____

_____

Make another meniscus. Touch it with the tip of your finger or with a pencil. Describe what happened.

_____

Student Inquiry Activity

This page will help you get your inquiry activity started. Use the Student Inquiry Worksheets for a guideline as you complete this inquiry activity.

A Meniscus on Your Mind

What is the largest meniscus you can make? _____

_____

_____

What is the highest meniscus you can make? _____

_____

_____

What is the best way to break the surface tension of water—alcohol, dish soap, cooking oil, or other materials? _____

_____

_____

Can you cover a meniscus with any kind of paper or material? _____

_____

_____

What ideas can you suggest for studying the meniscus?

    1. _____

    2. _____

    3. _____

    4. _____

Doing Your Inquiry Investigation

Use your Student Inquiry Worksheets to guide you as you do the following:

    1. Choose your inquiry question.

    2. State your hypothesis (scientific guess).

    3. Plan your investigation.

    4. Do the experimentation.

    5. Record your data and results.

    6. State your conclusions.

Unit 22

Wind

DID YOU KNOW THAT . . . ?

● *Winds in the polar jet stream around the Arctic can reach speeds of 200 miles an hour, more than twice the speed of some hurricane force winds.*

● *The Chinese invented kites to ride on the wind more than 2,500 years ago.*

● *The air pressing down on you weighs about a ton, but you do not feel it because it presses on you from all sides with equal force.*

MOVING AIR

Air never stops moving. Air carries water vapor and heat around the world. Wind is the movement of air throughout the atmosphere above Earth. Our weather is the direct result of constantly moving air in a variety of wind patterns. Moving air masses create winds because air pressure and temperature vary from one location to another.

HOW WINDS BLOW

Air moves from an area of **high pressure** to an area of **low pressure**. When you blow up a balloon and let go, air spurts out of a balloon where it is being held under high pressure to the lower pressure in the room. Warm air rises because it is less dense and less heavy than cold air. This movement of warm air creates an area of low pressure with less air. Cold air, which is heavier than warm air, sinks to fill the area of low pressure. This constant movement of air creates winds.

LAND WINDS AND SEA BREEZES

Winds are often created at the edges of oceans and lakes based on this movement of warm air. During hot, sunny, summer days, the land next to a body of water heats up more quickly than the water. Warm air rises from the land. This creates an area of low pressure. Colder air over the sea rushes in to fill the area of low pressure, and this creates a breeze. At night the land cools more quickly than the water. Cold air sinks over the land and flows out to the sea. The sea is still relatively warm because it doesn't cool as rapidly as land. The warm air above the sea rises and is replaced by the flow of cool air from the land.

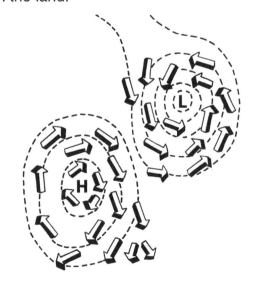

Wind

WIND DIRECTION

The **rotation** of Earth as it spins around on its axis affects the direction of major wind systems. Hot air moves north and south from the Equator to cooler areas. Earth spins from west to east, and major wind streams in the United States generally flow to the right from west to east. In other parts of the world, major wind systems called *prevailing winds* may flow to the east as they do at the North and South Poles.

MEASURING WIND SPEED

A windsock can show the direction and strength of the wind. When the wind is blowing fairly strong, the sock will fill with air and point in the direction the wind is blowing. Wind vanes often attached to the roof of a house show the direction of the wind. An **anemometer** is a device used by scientists to measure the speed of the wind.

windsock

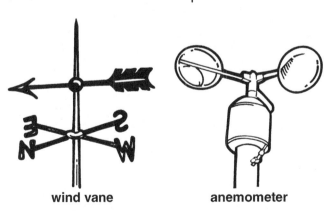

wind vane   **anemometer**

WIND POWER

Humans have used the power of wind for centuries. They created windmills to grind corn and other grains in earlier times. Many modern windmills are used to pump water from wells deep under ground. Today, huge farms of windmills are used in some areas of the world to run turbines that generate electricity. The pinwheels that are designed on the next two pages catch the wind in a way that is similar to the working of windmills.

Facts to Remember

● *Wind is created by moving masses of air.*

● *Air moves from an area of high pressure to an area of low pressure.*

● *Warm air rises; cool air sinks.*

● *The rotation of Earth affects the direction of winds.*

VOCABULARY

anemometer—*a device for measuring the speed of wind*

high pressure—*an area with air molecules tightly pressed together*

low pressure—*an area with air molecules more loosely arranged*

rotation—*the spinning of Earth on its axis*

Making Pinwheels

Materials
- *scissors*
- *clear tape*
- *pins or pushpins*
- *straws or pencils with erasers*

Directions

1. Cut out the Model A pinwheel shown below. Cut along line segments A, B, C, and D.
2. Pull point A to the center of the square and hold it in place with a small piece of tape.
3. Pull point B to the center of the square and hold it in place over point A with a small piece of tape.
4. Pull point C to the center of the square and hold it in place over points A and B with a small piece of tape.
5. Pull point D to the center of the square and hold it in place over the other points with a small piece of tape.
6. Push a pin through the center of the model and into a straw or the eraser of a pencil.

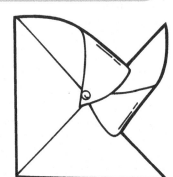

Using the Pinwheel

Hold the pinwheel outside in a breeze. Move it around in different directions until the wind catches the loops and whirls it. If the breeze is light, run with the pinwheel above your head.

Making a Different Model

Use the same directions to make the other pinwheel (Model E). Test it in the air. Which pinwheel works better?

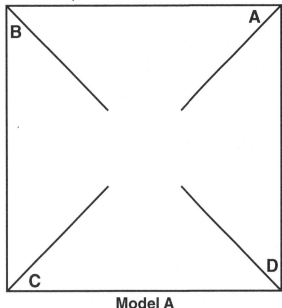

Model A

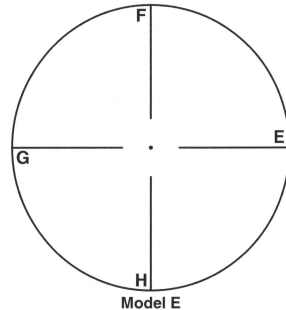

Model E

Making Windwheels

Materials
- *scissors*
- *clear tape*
- *water bottles*
- *straws, two sizes (jumbo and regular)*

Directions

1. Make two pinwheel designs. Use either of the designs on page 124 or make wheels of your own design.

2. Do not use pins.

3. Slit one end of the thinner straw as shown on the right.

4. Use clear tape to attach one wheel to the slit ends of the thinner straw.

5. Cut a 3-inch piece of the jumbo straw.

6. Slide the thinner straw through the 3-inch piece of jumbo straw.

7. Slit the other end of the thinner straw as shown above.

8. Use clear tape to attach the second wheel to the slit ends of the thinner straw.

Using the Windwheels

1. Hold the jumbo straw and face the wheels into the breeze. Adjust your position until both straws are moving freely. If the breeze is too faint, run in different directions until the wheels move freely.

2. Fill a plastic water bottle almost full of water. Put the cap on tightly.

3. Tape the windwheel to the top of the bottle as shown in the illustration.

4. Adjust the position of the bottle until the breeze is moving the windwheel. The filled bottle should keep the wheel from blowing over.

Try Again

Make a different set of wheels of a smaller or larger size. Which set worked better?

Student Inquiry Activity

This page will help you get your inquiry activity started.

Working with Wind

1. What is the best pinwheel you can make using any kind or paper or plastic?

   _____

   _____

2. Draw sketches showing some designs.

Testing Your Inquiry

How would you test each design?

_____

_____

Would natural wind, running, or a fan be better for testing each pinwheel design?

_____

Becoming a Windmill Engineer

- What is the best design for a model windmill? Sketch some designs in the space below.

- Which design would you choose to build? Why? _____

  _____

- How would you test the design? _____

  _____

Making Decisions

Use the Student Inquiry Worksheets to help you choose your pinwheel or windmill inquiry, plan your designs, and complete the investigation.

Helicopters

DID YOU KNOW THAT . . . ?

● *Helicopters are the most versatile of all flying machines.*

● *It takes both arms and both legs for a person to pilot a helicopter.*

WHY HELICOPTERS WORK

Air occupies the atmosphere above Earth. When any object is pulled to the ground by the force of gravity, the air pushes against the falling object and slows its fall. Many seeds have wings shaped like an airfoil that allows them to be carried on the wind as they gradually twirl toward the ground. These wings act like the rotors of the model helicopters on pages 129 and 130.

The wings and rotors spin and stir up areas of low pressure above them. Higher pressure from the air below keeps them in the air longer as they slowly fall to the ground. Real helicopters create areas of low pressure above them by the force of their spinning rotors. This area of low pressure helps create lift allowing the helicopter to take off into the air and remain there. The air is pushed downward, and this creates an opposite upward push against the rotors.

Helicopters are a very special type of aircraft. Helicopters are built with **rotating** blades fixed on top of the craft. These blades provide power, lift, and steering. They allow helicopters to move in many directions. Helicopters can take off vertically and hover over an area. They fly slowly and are capable of flying at either high or low altitudes.

SPECIAL FEATURES

Helicopters can do three things that traditional airplanes cannot do. They can fly backwards. They can hover. They can rotate in a complete circle in the air. Helicopter pilots use these special features for many tasks. A helicopter can literally sit in the air at the same place, while rescuers try to lift a stranded climber off a mountain pass or a boating accident victim bobbing on ocean waves.

The ability of the helicopter pilot to rotate his or her plane in a complete circle allows the pilot and passengers a full and close up view of fires, plane crashes, accidents at sea, traffic jams, and many other critical situations. Because helicopters can fly backwards, they can maneuver around dangerous mountains, between tall buildings, and fly into and out of tighter spaces than planes can.

Unit 23

Helicopters

PILOTING A HELICOPTER

Helicopter pilots have a very difficult job controlling all of the functions of a helicopter. A pilot uses one hand to move the **cyclic**, the control that determines the direction of the helicopter going forward, backward, left, and right. The pilot's other hand manipulates the **collective**, a control that determines the up and down motion of the aircraft. It also controls engine speed. The pilot's feet are used to push pedals that control the tail rotor, which allows the helicopter to swing around in a circle.

USES

Helicopters have many uses. Because they can hover and travel slowly, helicopters can be used for surveillance by police and military units. They can be used to fight fires by dropping water and fire-retardant chemicals. Helicopters are used for spraying crops with certain chemicals to protect the crops from insect pests. They are very useful to fire, police, and rescue groups because they can help get rescue teams onto mountains, along seashores, and into inaccessible, wild areas.

Facts to Know

● *Helicopter wings are designed to create lift when rotated rapidly.*

● *Helicopters can fly forwards and backwards.*

● *Helicopters can rotate in a circle and hover.*

● *The special design of a helicopter makes it very useful for rescue missions and emergency situations.*

VOCABULARY

collective—*the helicopter control which allows the machine to move up and down*

cyclic—*the control which allows a helicopter to move in any direction (forward, backward, left, or right)*

rotate–*to move around in a complete circle*

Making Helicopters

Materials
- *paper clips*
- *scissors*

Making Model A

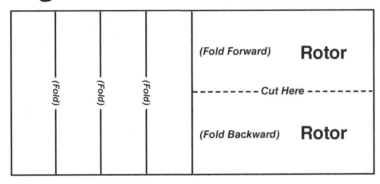

Model A

Final Product

1. Cut out the Model A helicopter.
2. Cut between the rotors.
3. Fold along the lines so that there are four overlapped folds.
4. Place a small paper clip over the fold.
5. Fold one rotor up and one rotor down.
6. Hold Model A by the rotors as high as you can. Let the model go. The model should twirl as it falls.

Making Model B

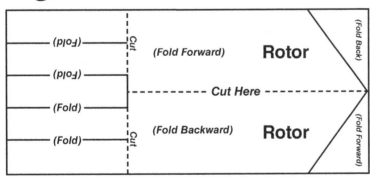

Model B

Final Product

1. Cut out the Model B helicopter.
2. Cut between the rotors.
3. Cut along the edge of each rotor where the model says "cut." Do not cut the center fold.
4. Fold along the lines on each side so that there are five overlapped folds in the center.
5. Place a small paper clip over the fold.
6. Fold one rotor up and one rotor down.
7. Fold the tip of one rotor in and the other out.
8. Hold Model B by the rotors as high as you can. Let the model go. The model should twirl as it falls.

Making More Helicopters

Materials
- *paper clips*
- *scissors*

Making Model C

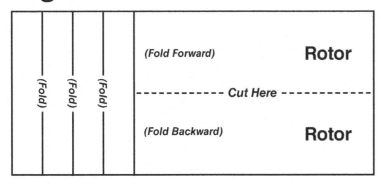

Model C

Final Product

1. Cut out the Model C helicopter.
2. Cut between the rotors.
3. Fold along the lines so that there are four overlapped folds.
4. Place a small paper clip or tape over the fold.
5. Fold one rotor up and one rotor down.
6. Throw Model C as high as you can into the air. The model should twirl rapidly as it falls.

Making Model D

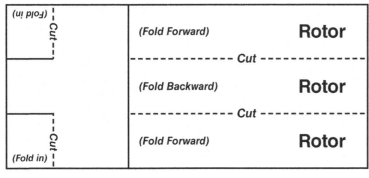

Model D

Final Product

1. Cut out the Model D helicopter.
2. Cut along the rotors.
3. Fold the rotors as instructed on the model.
4. Cut and fold the squares at the bottom of the model.
5. Place a small paper clip over the fold.
6. Hold Model D by the three rotors as high as you can. Let the model go. The model should twirl as it falls.

Student Inquiry Activity

This page will help you get your inquiry activity started.

Whirlybirds Away

What is the best paper helicopter model you can make? Draw some sketches below.

What tests can you perform to determine which paper whirlybird is best?

_____

Which design do you think will whirl faster?

_____

Which design will come down most slowly?

_____

Which design can carry a load—paper clips, stickers, or other material?

_____

Which design will whirl both on the way up and on the way down?

_____

What is the smallest working model you can make?

_____

Getting Creative

What inquiry questions about helicopters can you make and test?

1. _____

2. _____

3. _____

Making Choices

Choose your favorite inquiry question.

_____

Why do you want to investigate this question?

_____

What is your hypothesis (scientific guess)?

_____

Doing Your Investigation

Use the Student Inquiry Worksheets to guide you as you plan and do your investigation. Be sure to do several trials of your design and to record the results on the data page.

Principles of Flight

DID YOU KNOW THAT . . . ?

- *The first manned balloon flight was made in a hot air balloon launched in France in 1783.*

- *The first powered airplane flight was made by Orville Wright on December 17, 1903 at Kitty Hawk, North Carolina. The flight lasted 12 seconds. The longest of four flights that day lasted 59 seconds and went 852 feet.*

FOUR FORCES

An airplane of any type is affected by the action of four forces. These are *thrust*, *lift*, *gravity*, and *drag*. Two of these forces, thrust and lift, account for the ability of a plane to become airborne and stay airborne. Gravity and drag are the two forces that resist flight.

THRUST

Thrust is the forward force used to launch a plane into the air. In a jet plane, thrust is created by the power of the engine launching the plane into the air. The thrust needed to launch a paper plane is provided by the person who flips the paper design forward into the air. A plane with too little thrust does not get launched. A plane with too much thrust can end up crashing before it is airborne.

LIFT

Lift is created by the design of the wings. The wing of an aircraft is nearly flat on the underside and curved on the top. This special shape is called an **airfoil**. A bird's wing has the same shape created by the arrangement of the feathers. Lift occurs because air travels faster over the flat underside than over the curved upper side of the wing. The air has to travel farther and faster over the upper curve of the wing, and this produces less pressure than the air beneath the wing. Air pressure is reduced when the flow of air speeds up. Therefore, as the wing is propelled through the air, greater air pressure is created against the flat underside. With less pressure above, the wing and plane rise into the air. The faster the flow of air produced by the thrust of an engine or the arm launching a paper plane, the greater the lift.

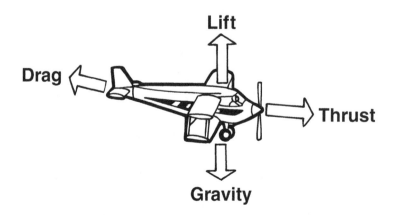

Principles of Flight

GRAVITY

The force of gravity creates a constant downward pull on the plane. *Gravity* is the force constantly pulling everything around us, including planes, toward the

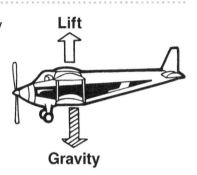

ground. When the lift generated by the speed of the aircraft and the design of the wings is greater than the weight of the aircraft, the plane rises and flies. When the force of gravity is greater than the lift, the plane falls. Paper planes will always fall to the ground because they get only one thrust as they are launched. The force pushing the plane through the air and helping to create lift is not renewed by an engine.

DRAG

Drag is the force created by the resistance of the air as the plane moves through the air. A plane or bird is constantly held back by the resistance of the air it is traveling through. Because air is real and powerful, any flying object must constantly push against the resistance of air. As an airplane travels faster through the air, drag increases. Drag increases faster than the speed of the plane.

Airplane designers are constantly looking for ways to reduce the force of drag and increase the force of lift. One way this is done is by **streamlining** planes. The body of a plane is designed with curved surfaces rather than sharp angles. When you design your paper planes, look for ways to reduce drag and the pull of gravity while you increase the forces of thrust and lift.

Facts to Remember

● *The four forces that affect flight are thrust, lift, gravity, and drag.*

● *Thrust is the force that propels a plane forward.*

● *Lift is the upward force pushing a plane into the air.*

● *Gravity is the downward force pulling a flying object toward the ground.*

● *Drag is the resistance of air against a flying object.*

VOCABULARY

airfoil—*a wing with a flat under surface and a curved upper surface*

streamlining—*using curved surfaces to reduce drag*

Flying Planes—The Cruiser

Materials
- *8 ½" by 11" paper*
- *ruler*
- *small paper clips*

Directions

1. Hold the paper vertically. Measure two inches from the bottom of the paper. Draw a line. (fig 1)

2. Fold the paper down to the two-inch line. Paper planes fly best when the folds are symmetrical, and most of the weight is in the nose of the plane. Make your folds neat and sharp. (fig 2)

3. Fold the paper in half down the center. (fig 3)

4. Then reopen and lay flat. (fig 4)

5. Lift one edge of the folded paper and fold a triangle along the center line. (fig 5)

6. Fold the opposite corner down along the center fold. (fig 6)

7. Fold the tip of the triangle at the top down to the two-inch line. (fig 7)

8. Fold along the center line again. (fig 8)

9. Measure one inch from the center fold on both sides of the model and draw lines. (fig 9)

10. Fold up along these one-inch lines. (fig 10)

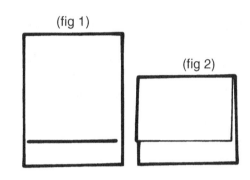

(fig 1)   (fig 2)

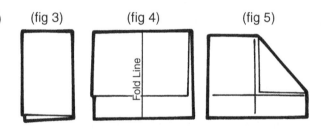

(fig 3)   (fig 4)   (fig 5)

Fold Line

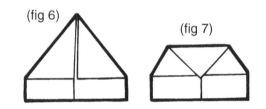

(fig 6)   (fig 7)

To fly the plane, hold the plane between your thumb and middle finger. Place your forefinger against the rear of the plane.

Launch the plane up into the air with a flip or snap of the wrist.

Try placing one small paper clip to each side of the nose of the plane.

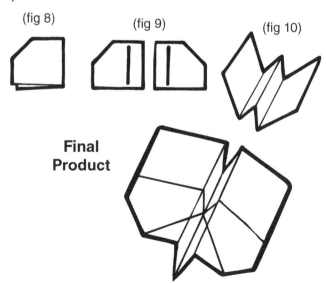

(fig 8)   (fig 9)   (fig 10)

Final Product

Flying Planes—Wide Body

Materials
- 8 ½" by 11" paper
- ruler
- small paper clips

Directions

1. Hold the paper vertically. Measure one inch from the bottom of the paper. Draw a line. (fig 1)

2. Fold the paper down to the one-inch line. Paper planes fly best when the folds are symmetrical and most of the weight is in the nose of the plane. Make your folds neat and sharp. (fig 2)

3. Fold the paper in half down the center. (fig 3)

4. Reopen and lay flat. (fig 4)

5. Lift one edge of the folded paper and fold a triangle along the center line. (fig 5)

6. Fold the opposite corner down along the center fold. (fig 6)

7. Measure and draw a line one inch from the tip of the triangle. (fig 7)

8. Fold the tip of the triangle down along the one-inch line. (fig 8)

9. Fold along the center line again. (fig 9)

10. Measure two inches from the center fold on both sides of the model and draw lines. Fold along these two-inch lines. (fig 10)

11. Measure one half inch from the edges on both sides of the model and draw lines. Fold up along these half-inch lines. (fig 11)

To fly the plane, hold the plane between your thumb and middle finger. Place your forefinger against the rear of the plane.

Launch the plane up into the air with a flip or snap of the wrist.

Try placing one small paper clip to each side of the nose of the plane. Try folding the rudders down.

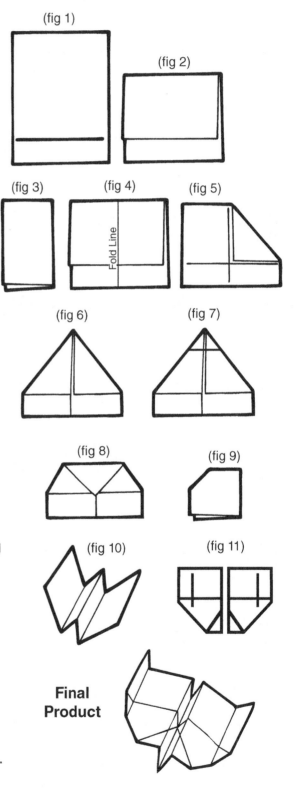

Final Product

Student Inquiry Activity

This page will help you get your inquiry activity started.

The Best Paper Plane

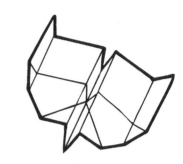

- How high can you make a paper plane fly?
- How far can you make a paper plane fly?
- How long can you keep a paper plane in the air?
- How many loops can you get a paper plane to make in one flight?

Getting Started

Make a paper plane model of your own design. Tell how you made it in steps.

Step 1: _____

Step 2: _____

Step 3: _____

Step 4: _____

Step 5: _____

Draw a sketch of the plane.

Choose one of the inquiry questions at the top of the page or make one of your own. Write it below.

Inquiry Question: _____

_____

Trials

Do several trials with your model. Record the results in terms of time, distance, or loops on the lines below.

Trial 1 Results: _____

Trial 2 Results: _____

Trial 3 Results: _____

Trial 4 Results: _____

Doing Your Inquiry Investigation

Choose an inquiry question about paper planes to investigate in detail. Use the Student Inquiry Worksheets to guide you as you plan and do your investigation.

Sound

DID YOU KNOW THAT . . . ?

- *Sound travels about 1,100 feet per second at sea level.*

- *Whales communicate using high-pitched sounds which other whales can hear hundreds of miles away.*

- *Some aircraft can fly much faster than the speed of sound.*

- *A sonic boom is created when an aircraft goes faster than the speed of sound.*

WHAT IS SOUND?

Sound is a form of energy produced by vibrating objects. These **vibrations** have two motions. First, vibrations push the air forward pressing the molecules of air together. The second motion pulls the air back causing the air to expand. These vibrations travel through the air as sound waves. The speed of sound in air is about 740 miles per hour depending on the temperature of the air and the altitude above sea level.

Sound waves can travel through air, water, wood, glass, metals, or any other material. Sound waves travel faster through dense materials with closely packed molecules. Sound travels about five times faster through water than through air. It can travel sixteen times faster through glass or iron than through air. However, sound waves cannot travel at all through a vacuum like outer space.

FREQUENCY

Sound waves traveling through air have different **frequencies** and different wavelengths. The frequency or pitch of a sound is determined by the number of vibrations in a single second. A sound which produces many cycles of compression

High-Frequency Sound Wave

Low-Frequency Sound Wave

and expansion in one second has a higher frequency than one which produces fewer vibrations. High frequency sounds have shorter wavelengths and more wavelengths than those of lower frequency. Frequencies are measured in standard units called **Hertz** which is abbreviated Hz. One Hertz is the speed of one wavelength every second.

Humans can hear sounds in frequencies between about 50 Hz and 20,000 Hz. Higher frequencies cannot be heard. Many animals including dogs can hear at higher frequencies than humans. A dog whistle has a frequency so high that dogs but not humans can hear it. Musical notes on an instrument have very exact measurements. For example, middle C has a precise frequency of 256 Hz.

Unit
25

Sound

HOW YOUR EAR HEARS

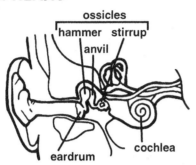

ossicles
hammer stirrup
anvil

cochlea

eardrum

Our ears collect sound waves. Human ears, like those of most mammals, have three distinct regions or parts. When sound waves enter a human ear, they travel through the outer ear as if through a funnel until they strike the eardrum. The waves of sound make the eardrum vibrate back and forth. The vibrations are then carried by three bones in the middle ear called **ossicles**. They make the sounds louder.

The vibrations are transmitted to the inner ear where the fluid in the inner ear called the *cochlea* starts to vibrate. These vibrations are picked up by very sensitive cells and are sent as electric signals along nerves to the brain that translates them into messages. The force of the sound as it travels through the ear can be twenty times greater than the original vibrations picked up by the eardrum.

PROTECTING THE EAR

Human ears can be severely damaged by bursts of extremely loud sounds or constant exposure to loud noises. The loudness of a sound is measured in **decibels**. Normal conversation is about 50 decibels. An orchestra makes music in the range of about 80 decibels. Thunder is about 110 decibels. Jet aircraft at takeoff can be as loud as 130 decibels and rockets produce 150 decibels.

Human eardrums can burst at 140 decibels. Regular exposure to sounds above 80 decibels will damage human ears. A broken eardrum will result in deafness until it has grown back. Diseases and damage can occur in the middle and inner ear as well. You should never put any object into your ear.

Facts to Remember

- *Sound waves are created by vibrations.*

- *The frequency of a sound is measured by the number of vibrations per second.*

- *Frequency of vibrations is measured in Hertz (Hz).*

- *Human ears transfer and magnify sounds.*

- *Loud sounds can damage human ears.*

- *Never put anything into your ear.*

VOCABULARY

decibel—*a measurement of the loudness of sound*

frequency—*the number of vibrations per second; sometimes called pitch*

Hertz—*the measurement of frequency in vibrations per second*

ossicles—*three tiny bones in the middle ear*

vibrations—*sound waves created by the movement of objects*

Hearing Aids

Materials
- *construction paper*
- *masking tape*

Directions

You need a partner for this activity.

1. Use a piece of construction paper about 9 inches by 12 inches to make a tube with an opening at each end about 2 inches wide.

2. Use a piece of masking tape to keep the paper from slipping.

3. Hold the tube with the opening over your ear.

4. Have your partner tap lightly on the outside of the tube. What did it sound like?

_____

5. Switch with your partner. You tap while your partner listens.

6. Tap on different sections of the tube from end to end. Where is the sound loudest?

_____

7. Whisper at the end of the tube. Can your partner hear the whisper? _____

Making Modifications

1. Take off the tape and twist the tube tighter so that the opening is only one-inch wide. Re-tape the tube.

2. Do the same activities listed above.

3. Describe the effects of the tapping and whispering with the thinner tube. What was the same and what was different? _____

Longer Hearing Aids

1. Use a piece of construction paper about 12 inches by 18 inches to make a tube with an opening at each end about 2 inches wide. Tape the tube in place.

2. Do the same activities listed above.

3. Describe the effects of the tapping and whispering with the longer tube. What was the same and what was different? _____

_____

Megaphones

Materials
- *masking tape*
- *construction paper*
- *cardboard tubes of many sizes*
- *tagboard, butcher paper, and papers of different thickness and texture*

Directions

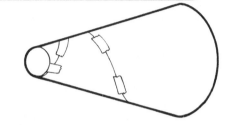

You need a partner for this activity.

1. Use a piece of construction paper about 9 inches by 12 inches to make a megaphone with a small opening at one end and a wide opening at the other end as shown in the illustration.

2. Use a piece of masking tape to keep the paper from slipping.

3. Speak into the megaphone. What does it sound like? _____ _____

4. Move five steps from your partner. Speak into the megaphone. Listen while your partner speaks into the megaphone. What does it sound like? _____ _____

5. Move ten steps from your partner. Speak into the megaphone. Listen while your partner speaks into the megaphone. What does it sound like? _____ _____

6. How many steps from each other can you get and still hear each other clearly? _____

Making Better Megaphones

Use different objects to create other megaphones of different shapes and designs. Try long cardboard tubes from paper towels or wrapping paper. Try using much larger paper, like butcher paper, to make larger megaphones with wide mouths. Use tagboard, a manila folder, or materials of different textures to create a megaphone.

Record Results

Illustrate each of your megaphones and describe how they worked.

1.	2.	3.

Student Inquiry Activity

This page will help you get your inquiry activity started. This investigation works best with a team of two students.

Materials
- *yardstick or meter stick*
- *paper towel tube*
- *tin can*
- *paper megaphone*
- *long wrapping paper tube*
- *long paper megaphone*

Directions

1. Find a place outdoors where you can shout.

2. One partner should shout as loud as possible.

3. The other partner should stand as far away as possible and still hear the words clearly.

4. Use yardsticks or meter sticks to measure the distance between the partners.

5. Try the same experiment with different types of cardboard tubes, paper megaphones, and cans with both ends off.

Inquiry Questions

- How far can you shout and be heard?
- What is the best megaphone design?
- What materials work best to make sound louder?
- How can you make sound travel longer distances?
- Can you get a string, wire, fishline, or stick to carry sound?
- Does weather affect how far sound travels?

Your Choice

Which inquiry question would you like to test? Why?

_____

_____

Making Decisions

Use the Student Inquiry Worksheets to help you plan your investigation, record results, and complete the project.

Brainstorming and Selecting a Science Investigation

Selecting a good science investigation requires some careful thought and serious planning. Follow these steps to help you get started.

1. Make a list of the topics in science that interest you.

   _____

   _____

   _____

   _____

2. List the science materials you like to work with, such as batteries and wires, animals or plants, flying or floating objects, chemicals or liquids, or any other similar science supplies.

   _____

   _____

   _____

   _____

3. List ideas for science investigations in every area of interest. Use textbooks, science experiment books, Internet Web sites, other sources, and your own ideas.

   _____

   _____

   _____

   _____

4. Make a choice of one idea for your project. Use this checklist to help you.
   Is the project interesting and different?

   _____

   Is the project difficult enough but not too complicated for you to do?

   _____

   Can you find or purchase the necessary materials?

   _____

   What support will you need from your parents in getting the materials or making the model or experiment?

   _____

   Have you used some of your ideas to make the project interesting and unusual?

   _____

   Do you have the time to do the project?

   _____

5. Name and describe your chosen investigation.

   _____

   _____

Displaying and Presenting Your Science Investigation

Make your science investigation stand out by following these suggestions.

1. Write neatly or use a computer to print out your written investigation.

2. Use proper spelling, grammar, and appropriate science vocabulary on your write-up. Use your own sentences. Do not copy from a book.

3. Have plenty of data for your investigation. Do several trials, models, or experiments to prove your results.

4. Display your project on a folding cardboard display unit, on tagboard, or use stiff art paper.

5. Illustrate your project with drawings, outlines, or photos to help the viewer understand what you did.

6. Label and demonstrate your models or materials used in the investigation.

7. Prepare an oral presentation for your classmates that gives all of the details of your work and the results.

8. Carefully and clearly organize and list the results of each trial, experiment, model, or survey that you did.

9. State your conclusions clearly.

10. Evaluate your project. What could you have done to make the investigation better, more detailed, or clearer?

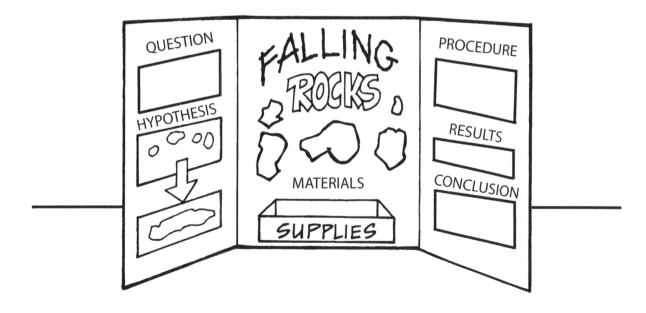

Science Investigation Format

Your investigation and display should follow the scientific method.

I. State a problem to be solved or investigated.

Examples: What happens to leaves without sunlight?

How does an electric circuit work?

What do mice really like to eat?

What colors make up white light?

II. Make a hypothesis (scientific guess) suggesting a possible solution to the problem or a plan of investigation.

Examples: Leaves need light to live.

Electric circuits must be connected.

Mice prefer peanut butter more than cheese.

There are several colors in white light.

III. Test your hypothesis using experimentation, models, and other investigations.

Examples: Cover several leaves on a plant for two weeks.

Create a variety of electric circuits.

Prepare a mouse diet and record mouse eating habits.

Use a prism and sunlight to refract light.

IV. Record your results.

Examples: Record the changes in the leaves every day.

Illustrate each electric circuit and describe whether it worked or didn't.

Keep a record of the mouse diet and what it ate.

Illustrate and describe the effect of sunlight passing through a prism.

V. State your conclusions.

Examples: Leaves can't survive without sunlight.

Electric circuits must be connected to a source of electricity and flow through conductors.

Mice prefer seeds more than peanut butter or cheese.

White light is composed of seven colors.

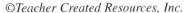